Principles
of
Macroeconomics

Principles of Macroeconomics

A.J. Rogers III

THE DRYDEN PRESS INC.
Hinsdale, Illinois

Copyright © 1972 by the Dryden Press Inc.
Library of Congress Catalog Card Number: 72-184502
ISBN: 0-03-089119-1
Printed in the United States of America

Preface

The series of which this book is a part has been constructed on an assumption that we all hope is correct. The assumption is that undergraduate instruction, and specifically the teaching of economic principles courses is no longer the stepchild of university curricula. There are certainly signs that this assumption is correct. Younger instructors with career commitments to teaching *principles* as well as research and higher level instruction are being put in charge of principles teaching and the structure of the courses. This type of instructor finds the massive classic hardback text less than satisfactory for the needs of today's students. True, many of these paperweights have the advantage that they come in a neat package of instructor's manuals, study guides, test banks, programmed learning work-books, graphics, film strips, etc., until hell won't have it—and neither will the conscientious instructor. The stuff is so pat, so canned, that any inno-vation on his part is lost in the shuffle or breaks the course program in a disruptive way. From the student's standpoint, the multi-revised, "up-to-date" denisons of the academic jungle are a real disaster. Their weight alone is enough to scare the average freshman or sophomore right into the nearest sociology course. When, and if, they actually start to read these jewels, students' original fear turns into sheer panic. I'll wager that there are more used economics principles texts with virtually uncreased spines than any other category of freshman course book.

There is nothing really startling in the series that we have put together. Our purpose has been to give an instructor some choices of material to be presented in the different segments of the principles course. To accomplish this, both the micro and macro portions have been divided somewhat arbitrarily into three segments each. Microeconomics has been split into *trade, markets,* and *microeconomic issues.* Macroeconomics has been divided into sections on *money, aggregates* or *macroeconomic analysis,* and *policy issues.* Within each of these six fields, three short paperback books have been prepared. The three books represent different approaches and different levels of difficulty. As you can see in the outline below, the lowest levels are all entitled "Elements of . . . ," the intermediate levels

	MICROECONOMICS				MACROECONOMICS		
	Trade	Markets	Issues	Money	Aggregates	Issues

Trade	Markets	Issues	Money	Aggregates	Issues
1. Elements of Trade 2. Principles of Trade 3. Theory of Trade	1. Elements of Markets 2. Principles of Markets 3. Theory of Markets	1. Elements of Microeconomic Issues 2. Principles of Microeconomic Issues 3. Theory of Microeconomic Issues	1. Elements of Money 2. Principles of Money 3. Theory of Money	1. Elements of Macroeconomics 2. Principles of Macroeconomics 3. Theory of Macroeconomics	1. Elements of Economic Policy 2. Principles of Economic Policy 3. Theory of Economic Policy

"Principles of . . . ," and finally the highest levels "Theory of . . . ." This use of titles is designed to keep potential confusion between levels at a minimum.

Generally, books in the upper or "Theory" level are heavily analytical in approach and use algebra, geometry, and simple set theory. Books in the intermediate or "Principles" group are aimed at approximately the level of a standard principles text. Simple algebra and geometry are the most sophisticated tools of logic used. The lowest level uses only the very simplest geometry and descriptive material for development of the analysis. None of the books employ much institutional material nor present many straight facts and figures. This we leave to the instructor whose taste for his own materials is likely to be far more effective in teaching than any material we could include.

The whole idea of the series is to give the instructor a chance to *vary* the level of difficulty and method of approach between the several sections. Thus, for example, an instructor might choose the intermediate level for all phases of the course except *money*, where he might wish to use the higher level. We expect a great deal of substitution between the "Elements" and the "Principles" levels. Similarly, we expect a considerable amount of mixing between the "Principles" and "Theory." I doubt if there will be much mixing between the top and bottom levels within the same course although there is certainly nothing to prevent such a mix. Any six books chosen from each of the segments will make a coordinated package covering the complete range of a two semester principles course.

There is a certain amount of overlapping and repetition between the books, and this is intentional. In the first place, it is hoped that many of these books will fulfill the function of supplementing other materials in principles and intermediate courses. But even when used as primarily intended, the overlap provides emphasis and review of the most important concepts developed elsewhere.

In all of the books, there has been an attempt to keep the style as light as possible. Those that think that textbooks should read like journal articles will be very unhappy with this aspect of the series.

One of the key features of this approach is the fact that portions of the series can be quickly and economically revised as the contemporary scene dictates. The system employed by Dryden Press in producing this group of books makes it possible to go from manuscript to finished product in two months. We are living in a revolutionary age when it comes to the passing of information. The authors hope that our approach will take advantage of some of the potential this revolution makes possible. Obviously, your constructive comments will be most welcome. If this product is not exactly what you want, tell us. By maintaining close two-way communication, maybe we can all do a better job of developing a measure of understanding about the world of choices in which all of us, teachers and students, live.

A.J. Rogers, III   Milwaukee, Wisconsin
General Editor   December, 1971

Contents

	Preface	v
Chapter One	Introduction	1
Chapter Two	Markets	19
Chapter Three	Aggregate Demand	41
Chapter Four	Aggregate Supply	51
Chapter Five	The System	63
Chapter Six	Governments and Foreigners	73

Principles
of
Macroeconomics

Chapter One   Introduction

This is a book about macroeconomics. It is a simple book that is intended to give you a bit of insight into the forces operating within the whole economy that make the thing either work or work not so well. You certainly will not become a "professional economist" (whatever that might mean) by completing the study of this tome, but it just might get you to start asking some embarrassing questions of people who claim to be economists.

Certainly, if we are to maintain anything that approaches a free society, it is imperative that our citizenry gain enough knowledge of economics to prevent politicians and special interest groups from conning us all. Checks and balances is the name of the game for any community where individual liberties are one of the things to be maximized. As you have already read, the operation of a free market can provide some automatic checks and balances when it operates without concentration of power.

If the market system would operate without imperfection, this portion of the study of economics would be only of passing interest as a mental exercise. However, in the "real world" the market *does* have imperfections. As a result of these, people begin to tinker with individual markets as well as factors that affect the whole machine. Because of this fact of live, the study of how all the bits and pieces fit together would no longer be a mental exercise; it is, in fact, an area of essential knowledge if you are attempting to be in a position to act rationally and as a responsible participant in the whole operation of living.

Where does it all come from? All material goods and services we take for granted in our everyday life must be produced somewhere, sometime, somehow, and by someone. This simple fact of life is just as true in Communist China as it is in Russia, Britain, or the U.S. No matter what your study of economics has consisted of up to this point, there is at least one thing you must have learned. There are no free lunches. (There may be for you, but there never is for the whole system in which you life.) An *economic good* is defined as something which first of all yields positive services to the user, and in addition, requires the user's giving up something else of value. In other words, an economic good is, by definition, something that is *scarce*. A resource of some kind had to be used to produce it and therefore, that resource was not available for some alternative production. In short, in order for someone to *consume* or *use* something, that something had to be *produced*.

It is true that there are some things which society can use without cost—without giving up something else. For example, as I am writing this manuscript, I am sitting on a sailboat in a small harbor in northern Michigan. I am "consuming" several things without apparent cost to either myself or the community in which I live. For one thing, I am breathing. Each breath I take uses some of the magnificently fresh air. But here there is sufficient fresh air so that my breathing in no way detracts from other people's ability to also breathe fresh air. (Note that for me the air is *very* productive indeed; without it, I'd be dead within a few minutes.) Yet right here, the air is not scarce. I can use all I need and want without giving up a thing except the few calories of food energy required to make my lungs work. More important, not only do I not have to give up anything, but no one else in the society has to sacrifice anything either. The air is a *good* in that it is productive. It is a *free good* in that nothing must be given up to get it. How about that same breathing operation in the middle of Gary, Indiana on a day when the wind is blowing about 2 knots out of the northeast? It is true that one can still breathe, but to get fresh air in that location and under those circumstances would require a considerable expenditure of resources in the form of filters, air conditioners, and shelters to keep the crud out. Now fresh air is no longer a *free good*; it is an *economic good*.

Economists are notorious for using pictures, diagrams, and graphs to make their point; and I'm no exception. Figure 1.1 shows the idea of a closed system in its simplest form. Everyone in a society is a consumer in some way or they will not stay alive very long. Most people in a society also produce something during their lifetimes. These two functions are tied together in a circular flow that must exist. There is no getting out of it. Even Robinson Crusoe was faced with scarce alternatives in the use of his time. Even in that simple society, he both produced and consumed. His production involved choices between alternatives which used scarce time, and only if he *produced* could he consume.

Almost all texts on macroeconomics start out with the concept of the flow between the functions of consumption and production of economic goods as illustrated in Figure 1.1, and with very good reason. However, this concept can be usefully expanded, particularly in today's world with all of the revived interest in so-called *natural resources*.

What does the production process actually involve in its most general sense? Economists call anything that is used to produce something else a *factor of production*. There are many ways to break down factors of production, but for our discussion we will start with the categories of *labor* and *capital*. As we progress, these two broad categories will be broken down into more specific items.

The first such breakdown is to separate natural resources from all other kinds of capital goods. By *natural resources* or *natural capital*, we mean goods which are depletable. Once they are used, there is no way to replenish or replace the specific item. If very strictly defined, there are few things in this world that truly qualify for the title of natural capital. Oil, for example, is usually considered to be such an item, yet even crude oil can be produced by laboratory techniques. Of course, were it necessary to

Figure 1.1
The Circular Flow

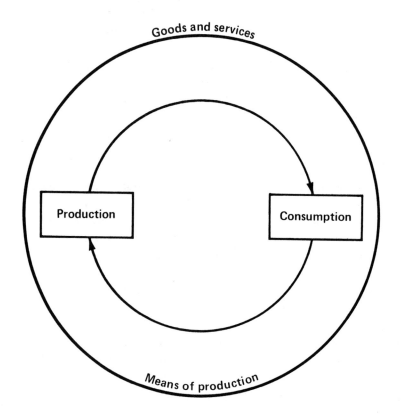

obtain our petroleum in this manner, and *at this moment in time*, it would not be economically feasible. There are substitutes which could perform the many functions of natural petroleum at a smaller resource cost than producing it from carbon, hydrogen, and oxygen.

The economic reasoning for separating natural or depletable capital from other capital is this: At any given time, the specific technology available implies that certain resources going into production processes, once used, will never be available again. This does not mean that we have to panic and despair the fact that this or that resource is going to disappear from the face of the earth. But it does mean that certain inputs to the production processes must be viewed as having a finite limit which man cannot realistically expand.

In a rather far out sense, the real limit facing man is not the narrowly defined material one, but rather it is the limit of *useful energy*. In a very real sense, man's primary effort always has been expended in trying to find new sources of energy and better ways to harness existing sources. Whether his own muscle power or from an atomic pile, energy has been and continues to be one of the two ultimately scarce items. The other is, of course, time. As long as man desires to live and is denied eternal earthly life, *time* will be an economic good.

As far as our circular flow is concerned, it is useful to consider *some* type of depletable inputs going into the system. It is the first of several "tanks" which feed the process of goods and service creation. Corresponding to this input, there are leakages of used and waste products unable to find employment in the production of other goods. Therefore, injections from the natural resources reservoir are constantly required. To the extent that recycling of waste products is possible, fewer inputs are required. To the extent that population pressures build, more resources are required. This is illustrated in Figure 1.2. The point to be remembered about this particular reservoir is that natural capital inputs are, by definition, depletable inputs. The reservoir cannot be refilled except by the discovery of new sources or by the substitution of different resources. Historically, man has been able to do this to an amazing degree, but he can ill afford to forget that natural inputs have finite limits that must be reckoned with.

The second type of reservoir we will touch on at this point is the accumulation of goods into what are called *inventories*. In this case, the inventories consist of *consumer goods* and *capital goods* that are produced and held for sale at some future time. This is done for a variety of reasons

Figure 1.2
Reservoirs in the Economy

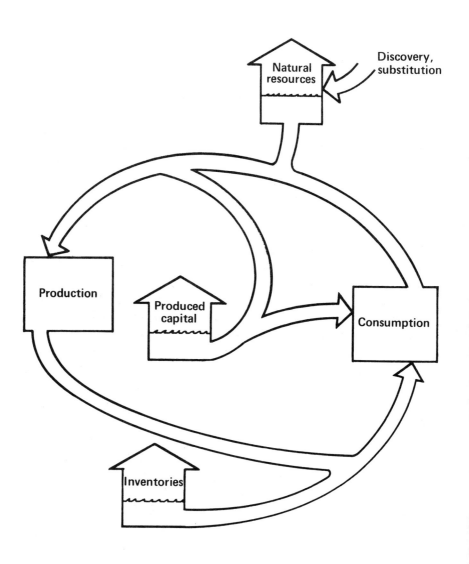

but primarily to gain a better utilization of productive facilities. Many products have a very irregular or cyclical demand over time. In order to have production facilities able to handle peak demand, firms would require plants of much larger scale which would then be operated only part of the time. On the other hand, smaller plants can be efficiently operated on a full-time basis and the excess product stored in times of slack demand to be used during periods of peak demand. Inventories, therefore, form a reservoir of goods between producers and consumers as illustrated above in Figure 1.2.

Finally, goods are used to produce other goods. These form our category of *produced capital*, which is also illustrated in Figure 1.2. Note that some capital is used directly by consumers. So-called *consumer durables* are such items as automobiles and major appliances. Other capital goods are used up in the production process. They *depreciate* or are partially used up by the process of making something else.

Since presumably you have already covered the subject of money, you therefore know that all of the flows covered in Figure 1.2 have counter-flows of *money* that is used to perform the necessary transactions. Thus, as the *real* flow of factors of production goes from the consumption sector to the production sector, money flows back from the producers to the holders of factors. This money then becomes the *purchasing power* which buys the output of the production sector.

As most of you know, attempts are made in this country and most other industrial countries to estimate the money value of the flows described above. The whole concept of national income accounting is to put numbers on the dollar flows which are proxies for the real flows. Thus, *Gross National Product (GNP)* is an estimate of the dollar value of all *final production* in the U.S. in any given one year period. Again, it estimates the value of the flow of goods and services in the economy. When one hears that the value of GNP was one trillion dollars, this means that over a one year period final goods and services valued at one trillion dollars were produced. Notice I have been saying the value of all *final goods* and *services*. An attempt is made in constructing the accounts to eliminate "double counting." For example, a contractor builds a house and sells it for $30,000. But the contractor had to pay a millwork company $5,000 for doors, windows, and trim. He paid a subcontracting firm $10,000 for carpentry, and another sub contractor $2,000 for other trades work. Finally, he paid various other suppliers a total of $10,000, thus leaving $3,000 as the amount he added to the product through his efforts. In an accounting sense, this was his "gross profit"; but in an economic sense, this was the amount the market paid him for the services his operation contributed to the total value of the house. This is the amount that would be added to GNP by the contractor's operation. The other items would be included in GNP as well but as the several totals of other operations building up to the final product. If each step of the way, the total sales value of the intermediate products were included, then double counting would result and GNP would be very much higher than the true value of production. As another example, when a tree is purchased "on the stump," this is one item in GNP. The lumber company that cuts the tree adds the tree cost to the cost of their services in delivering the tree to the mill. The mill takes its cost and adds to the price of the finished lumber. The window manufacturer would do the same thing. At each stage of the game, the original cost of the tree would be included *plus* additions to value made by the several processes. As you can see, this would highly inflate the true value of the final lumber. Even with careful attempts to eliminate double counting, our GNP figures still include a regretably large but unmeasured amount. This is but one of the criticisms of national income accounting.

Any industrial nation uses tremendous quantities of capital goods in their production processes. Part of this capital is used up each time something is produced, or in some cases, as time goes by. Therefore, the national accounts include an item for depreciation of the productive capacity of the country. Subtracting this depreciation estimate from GNP gives us *Net National Product* or *NNP*. NNP is an estimate of the market value of all production after allowing replacement of used-up capital. This then represents the market value of what is sold in the economy. From this figure, payments *other than* those made to factors of production are subtracted. Bad debts, sales taxes, and profits or losses from government enterprises are all removed resulting in the value of national product paid out to the factors of production. The value of *product* has now become the value of *income*, and in fact this item in the accounts is called *National Income*. Subtracting Social Security payments made to the government, corporate taxes, and then adding gifts and transfer payments made by governments and businesses back to individuals results in a category called *Personal Income*. From Personal Income, personal income taxes are subtracted and this yields the purchasing power of individuals in the economy. This then can be spent on either consumption expenditures or saved

Table 1.1   NATIONAL INCOME ACCOUNTS

Gross National Product

    — Depreciation

= Net National Product

    — Business Transfers (bad debts of persons and corporations)

    — Indirect Taxes

    — Profits of Government Enterprices (+ or —)

= National Income

    — Social Security Payments (contributions?)

    — Withheld Corporate Profits

    + Business and Government Transfers

= Personal Income

    — Personal Taxes

= Disposable Personal Income

    Consumption Expenditures

    Personal Saving

and invested. Table 1.1 shows a simplified breakdown of the major accounts.

There are many faults in our present measurement of GNP. Some of these faults are mechanical and may well be corrected in the future. Other problems, however, lie in the interpretation and use of national income data. It is important that some of these difficulties are understood. First, does GNP give us a useful measure of well-being in the economy? By itself, it most assuredly does not! GNP is expressed in current dollars. In other words, the value of goods and services produced is expressed in terms of the market prices prevailing at the time. Therefore, it is easy to see that if the GNP in the country goes up by 4 percent in a year while in the same year, the general level of prices increases by 6 percent, for instance, then the actual output in the economy has fallen, not risen. It is perfectly simple-minded, right? Sure it is, but look at how politicians might use GNP figures. If you are trying to show that your opposition has done a lousy job, you would point out this simple little fact. On the other hand, if you are trying to show what a magnificient job the government has done in stimulating economic activity, just use the raw figure. Of course, GNP can be "deflated" for price increases and expressed in dollars of constant purchasing power. This can reduce this particular problem.

Another problem of a similar nature is the fact that GNP does not take population into account. Straight GNP, or even deflated GNP, can be increasing by some percentage each year; but if the number of people in the economy is going up even faster, this apparent increase in well-being turns out to be a decrease. "Well," you say, "that's simple enough. Just divide the total deflated GNP by the total population and get a figure representing deflated *GNP per capita*. Now we have the problem solved and this figure should give us a useful measure of increases (or decreases) in the material well-being of our population." Wrong again! All the problems discussed thus far have been interpretive, but now we come to a more serious fault. In 1971, the country with the highest per capita income in the world is *not* the U.S.A., Great Britain, France, or Sweden; the highest per capita income in the world exists in the sheikdom of Kuwait. While I have never visited Kuwait, from the information available there is little question about the comparative material well-being of the average citizen there to the average citizen in almost any western nation. The hooker, of course, is that Kuwait gains tremendous revenues from its oil production. It is a tiny country, and when the small population is divided into the enormous oil revenues received each year, the per capita figure is impressive indeed. Of course, most of the revenue actually goes to a handful of people, rather than the general population. I am not suggesting whether this is good or bad, but the fact of the matter is that average per capita figures do not tell a thing about the *distribution of income* in the economy. It is perfectly possible (and it happens in many underdeveloped countries) that per capita income is increasing while the majority of the people have less material goods than previously. There is no simple way to correct this problem in national income accounting. The construction of *Lorenz Curves* can help, and this will be discussed in the policy book in this series.

Another major defect in the accounts is the fact that only *market transactions* are included. In a country such as ours one would think that this problem would not be very large. Practically all transactions take place through a market of some kind, right? Wrong again. How about all of the labor performed in the home by housewives and sometimes even children? This amounts to substantial quantities of output that are not even considered in the scheme of GNP. Changes in this output are also significant as households become more and more capital intensive in their operation. The net result of this fault is to *understate* GNP even in a highly market-oriented economy.

This problem becomes even more serious when national income accounting techniques are applied to underdeveloped countries. In these cases, it is not at all unusual to have a major portion of economic activity take place completely outside the marketplace. Thus, when you hear of a country with only $75 of buying power equivalent per capita per year, remember that in all probability most of the subsistence items are not even included. Much of this is produced and consumed without going anywhere near a marketplace which would measure the value of the product. Again, this is not to say that many underdeveloped countries are not in bad shape, at least materially. It does, however, say that often their material problems are overstated by the use of GNP figures. This has an even more serious ramification when viewing the improvements in the material prosperity of these areas. If GNP per capita went from a dollar equivalent of $75 to $100 in one year, everyone would cheer and talk about the great increase in well-being of 33 percent. In many cases, this apparent increase in output per capita is nothing more than an expansion of the market to include transactions that were formerly ignored or carried out using barter.

The depreciation item which is supposed to allow replenishment of productive capital stocks is another category that has problems. At present, this depreciation figure is obtained primarily from the balance sheets of the industrial operations in the economy. But one of the major criticisms of this kind of accounting is the fact that often it understates the use of our environment. In other words, resources that are now used as free goods are depreciating without any proper recognition of the fact in GNP figures. When a river can be polluted by dumping too much crud into it, and neither the company nor their customers have to pay for cleaning it up, then the *cost* of the product is understated. Understating the cost is the same thing as saying that the net value of national product is *overstated*. The depreciation item which converts GNP to NNP is too small since it does not include depreciation of all of the resources used.

Another obvious problem is that GNP figures are completely dependent upon values set by the market as it operates, rather than as it would operate under perfect conditions. If markets were perfect, then the values set would truly reflect the consensus of the society regarding the many goods and services available. Given imperfections, however, GNP will make no distinction whatsoever between the worth of an army halftrack and a mobile health unit. Decisions of the government to make purchases of various types are only indirectly related to the desires of the people. They are related indirectly through political action rather than the more immediate and direct market operation. To the extent that market imperfections of this nature or any other nature exist, GNP will reflect the distortions.

A final cautionary note needs to be sounded; there are many items which GNP lists as consumption expenditure which probably should be shown as investment. Of particular importance is the handling of resources expended on education and other forms of human capital development such as health programs, rehabilitation, and retraining. To the extent that these programs are successful, the productivity of the beneficiaries should increase significantly, thus making the expenditure analytically similar to an investment. Counting this as consumption will overstate consumption expenditures in the accounts and understate investments. It means that the purchase of a new automobile for pleasure will be treated as similar to resources spent on a college education. There are similarities in the two outlays, but there are important differences too.

After all that nonsense, you probably will never read a GNP figure again without laughing about how stupid the whole thing really is. I hope this will not be the case. The intent of pointing out all the problems has been to get you to be critical of numbers that are all too often tossed around without explanation or qualification. If used carefully, national income accounts can be useful tools in figuring out what is going on in the economy. But their indiscriminate use can actually be dangerous in that wrong problems can be fitted with right answers unless extreme care is exercised.

There is one more tool that you have probably already mastered which now can be used to illustrate again the idea of a *constraint* or scarcity. This is the production possibilities curve and a brief review of this concept may help prepare you for the upcoming trial of analyzing the whole economy. Consider for a moment that we lump all goods and services (*except* poverty programs) in the economy into one big category. (You can define "poverty program" in any way you wish at this stage of the game.) In Figure 1.3, we graph the dollar value of all output in the economy except poverty programs on the vertical axis, and the dollar value of poverty programs is graphed on the horizontal axis. What this diagram tells us is that if all of the available resources of the country were fully employed in producing just goods and services *except* poverty programs, a dollar value of *oe* would result. On the other hand, if the economy were thrown 100 percent into poverty programs to the exclusion of all other output, the dollar value of such programs would be *oj*. The line *efghij* represents all of the combinations of poverty and non-poverty programs that the economy could achieve if all resources were fully employed in a combination of both enterprises. For example, at point *f* it would be possible to have *od* of regular output and have *ok* of poverty programs as well. Similarly, it is possible to have *ob* of regular output and *om* of poverty programs. All points of production upward to the right of the production possibilities curve are *not attainable*. You just cannot get there given the capacity of the economy. On the other hand, all points downward and to the left of the curve are entirely possible; but if production takes place in this area, it means that some factors are going to be underemployed or unemployed. The full capacity of the economy is not being utilized. For example, if the economy were operating at point *n*, there would be *nk* of regular output and *ok* of poverty programs. In this case, it would be possible to have the same level of poverty programs and still get *nf* more regular output. No, this is not something for nothing. It is something for using what you already have but are *not* employing fully.

Figure 1.3
Production Possibilities

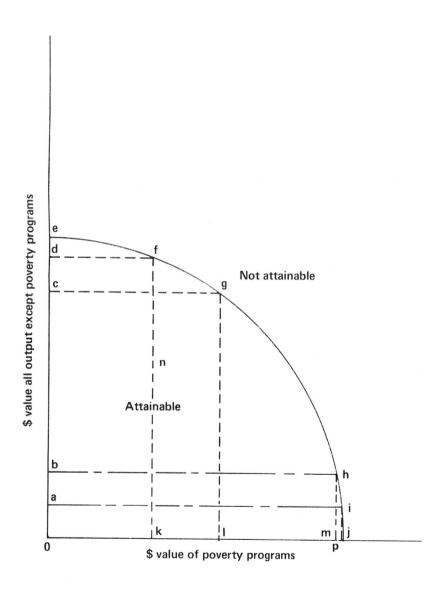

$ value of poverty programs

There is one other important characteristic contained in the diagram. Assume that the economy is operating at point *f*. Again, at this point there is a regular output valued at *od* and poverty program output valued at *ok*. If society decides to increase the level of poverty programs, it can do so in the amount of *k1* by giving up the production of *cd* worth of regular output. When the economy is approaching specialization in one category, getting more of the alternative is comparatively cheap. On the other extreme, however, giving up the same amount of regular output, *ba*, will allow only *mp* more output in the poverty program sector. When there is already a heavy output of poverty programs compared to non-poverty programs, the most efficient inputs are most likely already being used, and the transfer of more inputs to this field will not result in the same output increases. This general fact-of-life is well borne out by real world experience, and is often ignored by planners when they project the costs and benefits expected from various program expansions.

Economic growth can also be illustrated using the concept of production possibilities. In Figure 1.4 the boundary between attainable and non-attainable points has been shifted upward and to the right. Something has happened in the economy to increase its potential productivity. In the case of the U.S.A. such increases in productive potential have taken place due to improvements in available technology, as well as discovery and use of new resources. Given an outward shift such as this, it is possible to have more poverty programs and the same level of other output, or more regular output with the same level of poverty programs, or some more of both. In the diagram these choices are shown as a movement outward and to the right of point *a*. If all of the increased potential were taken as non-poverty program output, it would be possible to increase such output by *af* without reducing the existing dollar value of poverty programs. Similarly, were all of the increase taken in poverty programs, *ak* more programs could be instituted. Between these two extremes there are an infinite number of combinations all lying on the expanded curve *efghijkl*. Of course, expansion could also take place at the expense of one of the two alternatives. But again, society is constrained by resources and technology to the new production possibilities curve. Scarcity still exists, but with less intensity.

Before proceeding further, a word or two about the organization of the rest of this text would be useful. This presentation of macroeconomics assumes that you have covered the subject of *money* in some detail prior to attempting this portion of the principles course. If you have not, you

Figure 1.4
Economic Growth

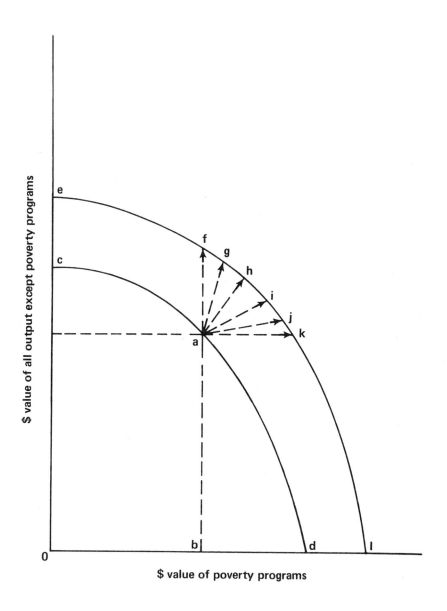

should find a money primer and brush up a bit. Needless to say, there are some fine paperbacks on the subject in this series.

Also, some of you may get upset by the fact that this particular book does not go deeply into policy issues. We mention a few things here to illustrate a point, but the main discussion on policy issues is again confined to another book in the series. Our purpose here is to acquaint you with some of the basic tools of analysis. Without these tools, you cannot go very far. With them, you should be able to understand some of what is going on in the country and even the world economy. Bear with it.

Chapter Two

Markets

Almost all economies in the world use either some kind of market system to allocate goods, services, and factors of production, or substitute some sort of planning body to perform the market function. If you have followed an outline similar to the one around which this series has been built, you have studied in some detail how markets operate and the concepts of supply and demand in individual markets. You should also have some idea of how imperfections in the market affect its operation, and a bit about how governmental bodies can operate on and through existing markets. All we are really going to do now is expand these ideas and combine many markets (conceptually) into a single set of interdependent markets operating together to form the total economy. We will use the basic micro tools of supply and demand, but modify them somewhat to accomplish the analytical task now at hand.

The markets we will be talking about are money, bonds, goods and services (we will lump services with goods from now on, since as you know, services are the only thing that make goods have value anyway), and labor. From these markets we will develop an aggregate demand function, an aggregate supply function, and show an aggregate market operation utilizing these two concepts. Three of these aggregate markets will be used to come up with an aggregate demand for all goods, and the fourth market, labor, will be plugged into an aggregate supply function.

The following is a review of some of the fundamentals that will be used in this discussion. Money is a good which provides several services. Like many other assets, it is a store of value over time and space. Unlike any other asset, money serves as a medium of exchange and unit of account by which unlike goods can be compared, or at least their values compared. The quantity of money demanded will vary directly with the general level of prices (*GPL*). Since the cost of holding money for transactions is the quantity of goods that therefore cannot be purchased at that moment, the price of money equals the reciprocal of the general level of prices. Hence, as with any other good, the Law of Demand holds, and the quantity of money demanded will vary inversely with its price. It will do so in such a way as to keep the purchasing power of money constant. Therefore, the demand for money will be a rectangular hyperbola relating the price of money (1/GPL) to the quantity demanded. This will hold as long as all other factors affecting the quantity of money demanded, such as the price of substitutes, bonds, level of output in the economy, etc., are held constant.

Bonds, in the sense used here, consist of any debt instrument which pays a return, or is supposed to pay a return. We generalize that the price of a bond is the amount one has to pay to obtain one dollar of interest income each year. Therefore, the price of a bond will increase as the rate of interest decreases, and vice versa. The price of bonds equals the reciprocal of the rate of interest.

How, then, will the price of bonds be related to the quantity demanded of money? As the rate of interest *increases*, this is the same thing as saying that price of bonds *decreases*. Since, as a store of value, bonds are a partial substitute for money, one can assume that a decrease in the price of a

Figure 2.1a
The Standard Demand Curve for Bonds

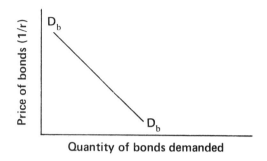

Figure 2.1b
Interest Rate and Quantity of Bonds Demanded

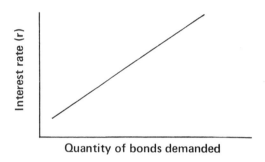

Figure 2.1c
Asset Demand for Money

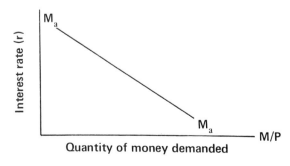

substitute will increase the quantity demanded of the substitute and decrease the quantity demanded of the given good. In our present case, this means that as the price of bonds falls, people will tend to hold more bonds and less cash for asset purposes. Of course, this makes perfectly good intuitive sense. If there is a very low rate of interest, you are much more likely to be satisfied holding cash at almost no risk as compared to making some kind of investment involving at least a small risk. In addition, cash is completely liquid, which is an advantage should you wish to spend your resources. Similarly, if interest rates are high, then the opportunity cost of holding money instead of bonds is also high, and there will be a tendency to hold less cash and more bonds.

In Figure 2.1a we show the standard demand curve for bonds. As the interest rate (r) gets higher, the price of bonds ($1/r$) gets smaller, and the quantity of bonds demanded increases. There is nothing strange in that situation. In Figure 2.1b, we have merely changed the vertical axis to represent the interest rate instead of the reciprocal of the interest rate. Now our *demand curve* for bonds is upward-sloping. Finally, we have drawn the quantity of money demanded as a function of the rate of interest in Figure 2.1c. As interest rates go up, the opportunity cost of holding cash goes up and the price of holding the substitute, bonds, goes down. Therefore the quantity of money demanded goes down. Sometimes this relationship is called the *asset demand for money*. It can also be called the liquidity preference function. Since this is a demand for money to be used as a store of value, the quantity axis is not just for a number of face-value dollars, but rather *real* or *purchasing power* dollars. This means that the axis should represent nominal dollars, *M*, times their price, *1/P*, or *M/P*. This is the real value of a stock of money, given different levels of price. This is just like the value of anything else; two dozen eggs at $.50 per dozen equals a value of $1.00. Again, as price goes up, *M/P*, the purchasing power of a given dollar bill goes down.

We have also said that money is demanded as a medium of exchange, and that the number of "purchasing power units" of money demanded to carry on transactions will vary directly with the level of output in the economy. The more transactions there are to make, the more *M/P* units of money will be demanded. If we graph this relationship, we come up with a representation such as Figure 2.2. Note in this case that the quantity of money demanded for transactions purposes may increase less than proportional output increases. This is empirically supported as well as expected from inventory theory.

Figure 2.2
Transactions Demand for Money

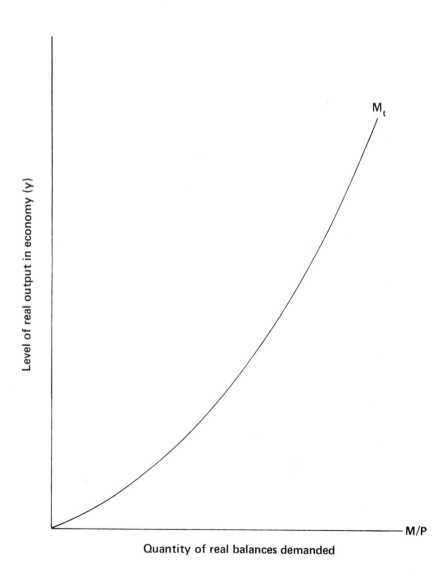

Quantity of real balances demanded

There is one very important fault in the analytical tools thus far developed. One could easily get the idea that there are separate demands for money for the two purposes thus far mentioned. There is *a* demand for money, and the two major components, *beside price*, have been made explicit. But money is money, and the transactions-demanded dollar is just the same as the asset-demanded dollar. In fact, the *same dollar* will be demanded for both purposes.

We have assumed the supply of money was controlled by the government, and that this supply was set independently of the price of money, which is the reciprocal of the general level of prices. Once we have a given stock of nominal money in the system, and some given level of prices, then the total purchasing power in the economy, M/P, is fixed. In Figure 2.3a, this amount is represented by the length of line *zo*. This total stock of money must be used either as a stock of money held for asset purposes, or a flow of funds being used to carry out transactions in the economy. In other words, if *a* amount is demanded for transactions, then *b* amount is left over and will be held as asset balance. The converse would be just as correct. If *b* were demanded for assets, then there would be *a* left over to circulate through the economy making purchases. If something happened to increase the quantity of money demanded for transactions, say, to *a'* (see Figure 2.3b), then the amount of the fixed stock of *M/P left over for assets would have to fall to b'*. The sum, *a* plus *b*, must absorb the total money stock. There is no other place for it to go.

If *equilibrium* is going to exist in the money market, at least two variables have to be just right. On an everything-else-being-equal basis, the asset demand for money will depend on the interest rate. Any particular quantity of money available for asset purposes will be willingly held only at a unique rate of interest. If the interest rate is higher than the equilibrium rate, people will try to dump money in favor of bonds. If the interest rate is lower than the equilibrium rate, people will try to get out of bond holdings and into more cash holdings. As far as transactions are concerned, a given level of real balances available for transactions purposes will be consistent with one and only one level of real output in the economy. If more funds are available than the equilibrium quantity, prices will tend to be bid up. An increase in the level of prices will tend to reduce the length of the line, i.e., to reduce the M/P available. Conversely, if there are too few funds available for transactions purposes, there will be a downward pressure exerted on prices. As prices fall, M/P gets larger. More real buying

Figure 2.3a
A Fixed Stock of Real Money (M/P)

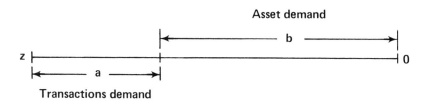

Asset demand

b

Transactions demand

Figure 2.3b
A Change in Relative Demands

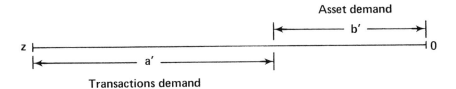

Asset demand

b'

Transactions demand

power is thus made available to reestablish equilibrium. Note that all of this assumes that prices are completely free to move either up or down.

If one portion of the demand for money is uniquely dependent on the interest rate, and another portion of the demand for money is uniquely dependent on the level of output in the economy, there must be a series of unique combinations of *interest rate* and *output*. This series would represent the possible combinations that produce equilibrium in the total demand for money. There is indeed such a series, and to visualize it see Figure 2.4. This diagram may look a bit complicated, but it is really not. Trace through the diagram each of the steps that are about to be described in the text. Do not try to just follow the text alone.

This diagram uses the total stock of real balances *zo* from Figure 2.3a, and again splits the stock and some arbitrary point *e* into a segment *a* which r epresents some level of real balances for transactions purposes. This leaves segment *b* for asset purposes. So far, nothing is changed from Figure 2.3a. Next, to determine the level of output to support a transactions demand for real balances of *a*, superimpose the demand for transactions balances on our line *zo*. It will have to be upside down to accomplish the necessary geometry, but this is no problem. In other words, the origin for transactions balance will begin at *z* and increase to the right. The level of output will also commence at *z* but this time it will increase to the south—downward. The function, M_t, is the same one as described in Figure 2.2. As the level of output increases, the quantity of real balances demanded for transactions purposes increases. Again, if segment *a* is demanded for transactions purposes, then segment *b* is left over for assets purposes. The question is, "At what rate of interest will people be willing to hold real balances in the amount of segment *b* for assets purposes?" To find the answer, again superimpose the relevant demand function for real balances, which in this case is the asset demand. This time we will use the *o* end of the real balance line as an origin and show increases in the balances demanded for assets purposes by a movement to the left, i.e., from *o* to *z*. The reasoning behind this construction is simple enough; the stock of money exists, it is given. Therefore, the stock must be absorbed for one of the two purposes. An increase in the quantity for transactions *must* be accompanied by a decrease in the quantity for assets and vice versa. By setting up our origins in this way, the graph shows precisely this situation.

From our asset demand origin, we construct an interest axis headed

Figure 2.4
The Demand for Money

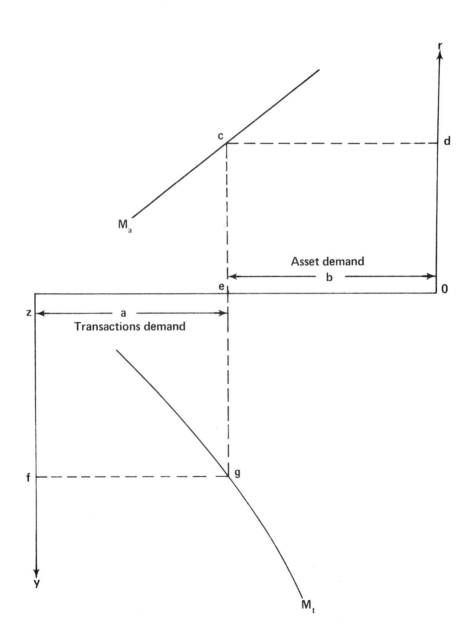

north—straight up. Increases in the interest rate are shown by movements in a northern direction, and decreases in the interest rate are shown by southern movements. Because of the location of the axis, the asset demand function slopes downward and to the left, but it is precisely the same function as was described in Figure 2.1. As interest rates rise, the quantity of money demanded for assets purposes decreases and vice versa.

We can now answer both the question of output level and interest rate that would be consistent with (1) a level of real balances equal to *zo*, (2) a transactions demanded quantity of *a* and (3) an asset demanded quantity of *b*. Segment *a* will be consistent with a level of output equal to *zf and only zf*. Segment *b* will be consistent with an interest rate of *od and only od*. Therefore, if everyone is to be happy (that is, in equilibrium) in the money market, there must be an interest rate of *od* if the level of output is equal to *zf*.

Now let's do a little fancy construction and see if we can construct all the possible combinations of interest rates and outputs that will be consistent with money market equilibrium. To do this, see Figure 2.5. It is no more complicated than Figure 2.4, except now we have added a couple of axes. Through origin *o*, another *y*-axis has been drawn parallel to the *y-axis through origin z*. The axis is labeled *y'* and values along it are identical with values along the *y*-axis itself. In other words, *zf* is equal to *of'*. Also through origin *o*, another *y*-axis has been extended to the east. Again, this axis has values of *y* exactly equal to those along *zy*. Thus, any value of *y* such as *f* on axis *zy* can be carried across the southwest quadrant to the *y'*-axis. Then, in effect, the *f'* value is rotated up to the *y''*-axis where it becomes *f''*. Therefore,

zf = of' = of''

At the same time, the value of the interest rate consistent with income *zf* was equal to *od*. The value of interest *od* is already identical for the northwest quadrant in which it was manufactured, and the northeast quadrant that we have just created. Next we simply plot the value of interest, *od*, with the matching value of output, *of''*, to get point *n*. Similarly, we can take any other arbitrary point on the *M/P*-axis which would represent a different combination of balances held for assets and transactions purposes such as point *s*. At this point the level of balance for transactions purposes has increased. In other words, the money left over for assets purposes has decreased. How would this new situation be consistent with

Figure 2.5
The Money Market

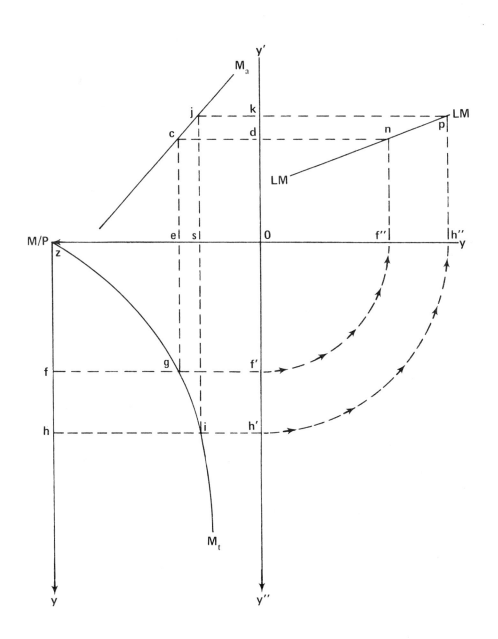

interest rates and levels of output? To begin with, larger balances for transactions will be used only if the level of output increases from *zf* to *zh*.
Carrying this value across and up gives us *oh"* in the northeast quadrant.
Simultaneously, the balances available for assets purposes have been reduced from *oe* to *os*. This will be consistent only with a higher rate of
interest. People will give up their holdings of cash balances only if the
alternative investments available yield a higher return. In this example, the
higher interest rate equals *ok*, up from *od*. Therefore, new interest rate *ok*
is consistent with equilibrium in the money market if and only if the level
of output in the economy is equal to *oh"*. The rest is obvious. Each
different combination of balances for transactions and assets purposes,
given the stock of real balances (M/P), produces a different set of
interest/income combinations. If all of these are plotted, we generate the
summary function LM-LM. So What?

The "so what," as I hope you will see shortly, is that we need some
kind of tie between the several markets that exist in the economy. In the
above example, we will need some kind of tie between the money market
and the market for goods. That tie is the interest rate. Hopefully, you will
be able to see this more clearly after the next section. In the meantime,
the *LM* function definitely makes intuitive sense.

This presentation has talked about four variables in the money market.
There are others, but those are being held constant for the moment. The
four under discussion are (1) the stock of nominal money, *M*, (2) the
general level of prices, *P*, (3) the level of real output, *y*, and (4) the rate of
interest, *r*.

To briefly summarize: If the nominal money in the economy and the
price level are held constant, then the purchasing power, or real balances in
the economy, are constant by definition. Given this constant level of
purchasing power, there will be no forces tending to change any of our
variables (equilibrium) only if higher levels of interest accompany higher
levels of output. The same thing could be said from the other side of the
coin. Equilibrium will take place in the money market only if higher levels
of output accompany higher levels of interest. The rate of interest and the
level of real output are directly related (one increases, the other increases)
if all other variables are held constant, and equilibrium is to be maintained.

One other point should be mentioned in passing for future reference
and use; just as with the supply and demand analysis of microeconomics,
the *LM* curve represents a schedule of values between two variables: inter-

est rate and output. If any other variable in the system changes, then the curve will shift its position. (You should be able to work out the geometry of this statement.) For example, if the nominal stock of money, and nothing else, is increased, then the real balances will increase. Line *zo* will get longer, and the origin *z* will move over to the left. This will mean that any given level of interest rate will now be consistent only with a *higher* level of real output. The *LM* curve will have shifted outward and to the right.

Try working out some of these shifts, such as an increase in the general price level, a decrease in the general price level, a decrease in the stock of nominal money, or an increase in people's overall desire to hold bonds.

Leaving the money world for the time being, we now take a brief look at the market which interests us all—the market for the things we use, the market for *goods*. There are two very broad categories of usage to which goods can be put. When one gains command over resources through income or gifts, those resources can either be used, i.e., *consumed*, or they can be *saved*. From this simplistic statement comes the first relationship we shall use: For the economy as a whole, the total output must find its way into consumption or saving. In symbols,

$$y = c + s \tag{1}$$

At this stage, we are talking about *real* values again. In other words, our y, c, and s, are measured in dollars so that we can have a common unit of account, but the measurement is in real dollars—purchasing power dollars. Because of this, changes in the general price level will cancel out and not affect the real value of any of these variables. It is the same situation as exists in our concept of real balances. Real balances give us constant purchasing power, and the real value of output gives us constant "purchasability."

Now comes a little identity which may give you a bit of trouble until you really think about it. I submit to you that anything that is saved is automatically "invested" whether the saver wants it that way or not. The resources thus invested may or may not produce a return for the holder, but once a saver does *not* consume some good, an investment has taken place. Again, in symbols, we are defining saving as being identically equal to investment, or

$$s = i$$

Next we make a simplifying assumption about the way people as a group act. The assumption is not completely correct, but it is sufficiently correct to produce results that are realistic and useful. The first of these assumptions is that the level of saving that people design and accomplish will depend solely on the level of their incomes—their real incomes. We assume that the level of saving is an increasing function of the level of income in the economy. Remember from the circular flow discussion that for the economy as a whole, *output* is the same as *income*.

Some may be quick to say that the level of saving will also depend on the rate of interest. They point out, and correctly, that at higher levels of interest, people will be willing and able to save more resources than will be the case at lower levels of interest. Again, they are probably right, but these factors will complicate the analysis at this point, and not change the results a bit. So again, the assumption is that saving depends on national output (income).

$s = f(y)$

As might have been expected, to see what other information we can get, this relationship is graphed in Figure 2.6. The graph is upside-down, again for reasons that will become apparent. The level of income is plotted from a righthand origin southward, and the level of saving is plotted from the righthand origin westward. The fact that we had said total output (income) must be either consumed or saved can be shown by constructing a 45° line through the origin. If the same dollar scale is used on the y- and s- axes, then any dollar value of y will reflect to an equal dollar value on s. In other words, if all income were saved, then the saving function would be the 45° line that is marked $c + s$ in the graph.

Of course, people do consume part of their incomes and save another part. By assumption (and in truth) as incomes rise, the amount of income saved increases. The way we have drawn the saving function indicates that the amount people save in the economy as a whole increases proportionally with increases in income. This relationship between the amount people want to save and the level of income is called the propensity to save. It is the fraction of total income that people will save. The *marginal* propensity to save is the fraction of each *additional* unit of national income that people will save. The *average* propensity to save is the fraction of *total* national income that people save.

If you remember the relationships between totals, averages, and marginals from microeconomics, you will recognize that the way we have

Figure 2.6
The Saving (Consumption Function

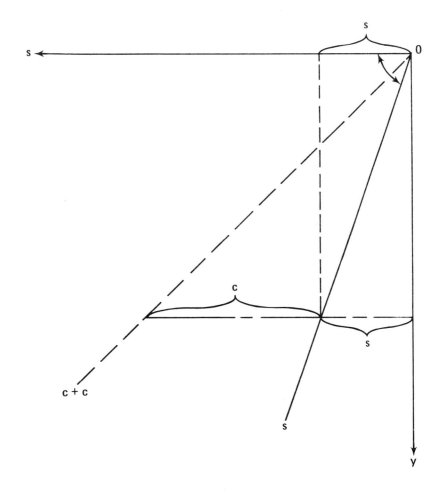

drawn the saving function, the marginal propensity to save is constant. The same fraction is saved of each additional real dollar of income. This means that the marginal propensity to save is equal to the average propensity to save. There is empirical data to support this hypothesis. This is not to say that different people with different levels of income have the same marginal propensity to save. It *does* say that the economy as a whole saves about the same fraction of its income over time.

There is another point that is obvious, but should be mentioned. With our simple definitions, with income going either into saving or consumption, whatever fraction of income is *not* saved becomes the fraction of income consumed. If we add the two fractions together, they must total one or the whole pie. For example, if the marginal propensity to save is .33, then the marginal propensity to consume must be .67 for a total of one.

There is one monumental area of confusion that often occurs when students begin their study of macroeconomics. This is the confusion between *stocks* and *flows*. The little model we are in the process of building describes a photoflash picture of an economy at an instant in time. Think of a river flowing just below a large dam. Behind the dam, there is a stock of water. Water flowing into the reservoir replenishes water that is flowing over the dam and into the river below. There is a stock of water in the reservoir. If you take a picture of the reservoir and the river, you will see the stock of water in the reservoir, and you will also see the flow of water in the river. The water in the storage will be measured in *gallons*. The flow in the river will be measured in gallons *per unit time*—gallons per minute or per hour, etc. The concepts of consumption and saving that we have been talking are about *flow* concepts. They are the *rate* at which people are spending on consumption or saving out of the continuing flow of production. There are, of course, stocks in the economy. We have already talked about the *stock* of real money, for example.

Another stock that can be confusing is the stock of savings. Note the difference: Saving is the rate at which people accumulate resources out of current production; savings is the result of that accumulation. *Saving* is a flow, whereas *savings* is a stock.

Remember again that every time something is purchased, that purchase becomes income for someone else. Because of this fact, when something is saved, that is, purchasing power acquired and not used, the demand for goods in the economy will go down. "But," you say, "if purchasing power is used to buy investment goods, this will again become part of the demand for total goods in the economy." Right you are if all of the saved resources are demanded by people who wish to invest. If *desired* saving equals *desired* investment, then there is no problem.

What is it that determines the demand for investment goods? The biggest single determinant will be the cost of making an investment. That cost, of course, is the interest rate that an investor will have to pay, either explicitly or implicitly, in obtaining investment resources. The higher the interest rate, the more costly will be the act of investment, or in other words, the more any investment project would have to return to make it worthwhile. Before we noted that saving, and therefore consumption, would depend on the level of national output (income). Now we see that investment demand for goods will depend on the rate of interest. Total demand will consist of both demand for consumer goods and demand for investment goods. In symbols we now have,

$c = f (y)$ and $i = f (r)$
and total demand for,
$y = c + i$

In Figure 2.7 the relationship between interest rates and the level of desired investment in the economy has been graphed. It simply shows what has just been explained; as interest rates decrease the level of desired investment goods will increase, and as interest rates increase the quantity of investment goods demanded will increase. The graph is again backwards, but this will be explained shortly.

Sometimes this function is called the *marginal efficiency of capital* (if you want to call it that, go ahead). It merely indicates that if the economy is going to demand more capital goods (goods for investment purposes), it will do so only at a lower rate of interest. The return on additional capital will be lower than that on existing capital.

Remember that actual saving must equal actual investment. Also remember that to have an equilibrium condition in the goods market, *desired* saving must equal *desired* investment. These two statements are not quite the same thing. In combining Figures 2.2 and 2.7 into Figure 2.8, we see just what is involved. Since saving and investment are the same number, we can combine the horizontal axis of both the consumption market (actually the mirror image, the saving market) and the investment

Figure 2.7
The Demand for Investment Goods

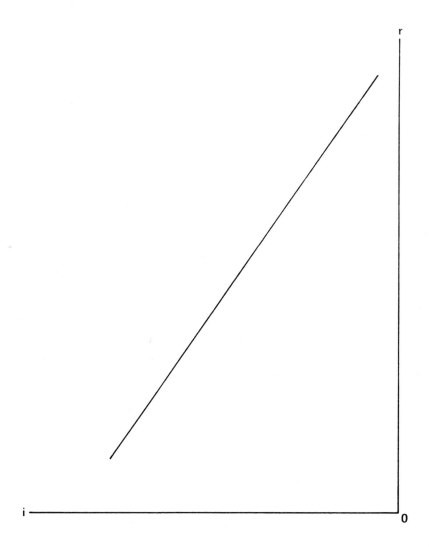

Figure 2.8
The Market for Goods

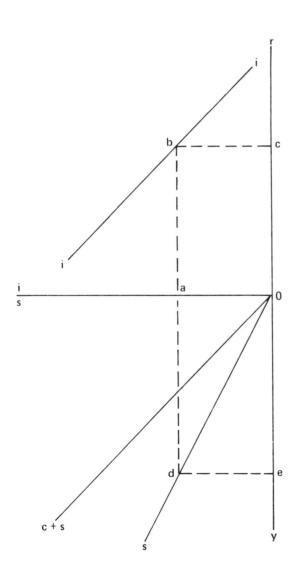

Figure 2.9
Construction of the Summary Function
for the Commodity Market

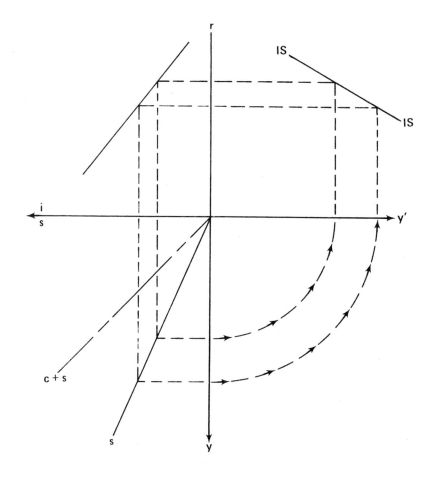

market. The top of the axis lying in the northwest quadrant is called investment *(i)* while the bottom of the axis lying in the southwest quadrant is called saving *(s)*. By constructing *i* and *s* with similar values, we impose the equilibrium condition that desired saving and desired investment are are equal. Now take any arbitrary value of *i* = *s*, say *oa*. People in the economy will be willing to save at this rate if the level of national income is equal to *oe*. That's one side of the coin. On the other hand, investors are willing to use that much investment capital if the interest rate is *oc*. Therefore, as before with the money market, there is a combination of interest rate and output which will bring about a demand for all the available output of the economy without pressures being exerted for change either in the interest rate or the level of output. As before, we can find all of the combinations of interest rate and output that are consistent with equilibrium in the market for goods. In Figure 2.9 this construction is illustrated.

The *y*-axis is rotated in Figure 2.9, or at least the values rotated from the southbound axis to the eastbound axis. By taking any arbitrary points on the *i=s*-axis, one can identify the unique interest rate and the unique level of output associated with the chosen point. By plotting these combinations of interest and output in the northeast quadrant, a summary function is obtained which is called the *IS* function. All it tells us is that for equilibrium to exist in the market for goods, increases in the level of real output demanded will be consistent only with lower rates of interest. Again, on an everything-else-being-equal basis, this makes perfectly good sense. Increases in the level of output available will mean that people will tend to save more, not necessarily a larger proportion of their incomes, but more real purchasing power nonetheless.

For this increased rate of saving to find a home, it is necessary for the rate of interest to fall in order to make the cost of investing capital lower. Looking at it another way, should interest rates fall from some given level, more goods would be demanded for investment purposes. Given the savings function (the mirror image of the consumption function), the only way those goods will be available is if the level of output increases.

Chapter Three

Aggregate Demand

Thus far we have seen the broad-brush operation of two markets directly (money and goods), and a third market because of its close relationship to money (bonds). But something interesting has come from all of the manipulations and geometry. We have derived a demand for money function relating interest rate and real output. We have also derived a demand for goods function relating interest rate and real output. In one of these (goods), interest is a decreasing function of output, and in the other one (money) interest is an increasing function of the rate of output. Clearly if the two markets are in the same economy, there must be an equilibrium between the two—and so there is.

Figure 3.1 combines a downward sloping *IS* curve and an upward-sloping *LM* curve. Where the two intersect, there is a unique combination of interest rate and real output which satisfies the equilibrium conditions for both markets. Notice, the caption of the illustration says that the bond market is in equilibrium too. This has to be the case since when two of three variables are fixed, and the total result of all three variables given, the value of the third must also be fixed. If there are three people drinking one fifth of Scotch, and two of the three gulp down a slug, the amount left over for the third is automatically set.

What would happen if the interest rate were other than the equilibrium rate *oa*, and output were other than equilibrium level *ob*? Assume that for some reason, interest was above the equilibrium rate. In the goods market, this means that desired investment would be less than desired saving so that the quantity demanded of output would be reduced from *ob* to *oe*. In the money market, the high rate means that people will reduce stocks of money held for asset purposes and purchase more bonds and goods. Money flowing into the bond market will tend to raise the price of bonds, which is to say that the interest rate will be depressed. Lowering the interest rate means that more goods will be demanded for investment purposes, thus increasing the quantity demanded of goods. Thus, there are movements along both the *IS* and *LM* curve back toward the equilibrium rate of interest and output demanded.

In the same manner, should the interest rate be too low as, for example, *od*, then the demand for investment goods in the goods market will exceed the quantity of saving people are willing to perform at the equilibrium level of output. In the money market, the low interest rate means the price of bonds is increased, making people more prone to hold cash balances instead of bonds or purchasing of goods. Again, both of these factors will tend to raise the interest rate back to the equilibrium level of *oa* and the equilibrium output of *ob*. Only at this combination of interest and output will the demand between the several markets be balanced.

Now it is time to derive an aggregate demand function for the entire economy. What does a normal demand curve usually represent? The usual demand curve in microeconomics represents the relationship between the *price* of some good and the *quantity demanded* of that good. It is constructed with the understanding that everything else conceivably affecting the quantity demanded of the good is held constant. Given this situation, we always have a negative slope demand curve. This fact is so general that

Figure 3.1
Equilibrium in the Demand for Money, Bonds, and Goods

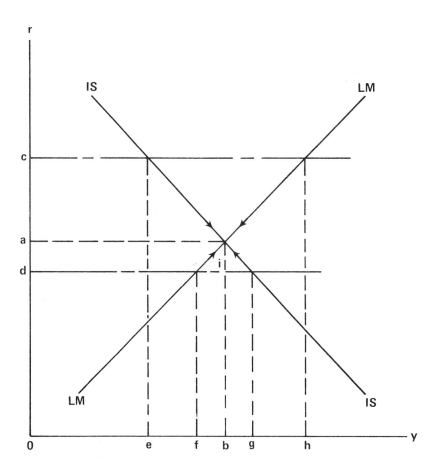

we call the phenomenon *The Law of Demand*. As the price of a good decreases, *ceteris paribus*, the quantity of the good demanded will increase. Among the usual things that are held constant are the prices of substitute or complementary goods, the incomes of the demanders, expectations of future events, tastes, and transactions costs.

When all the goods in the economy are added together, and then the money and bonds markets are thrown in as well, the things held constant along the demand function change somewhat. But we can still develop an aggregate demand curve for the entire economy that is very useful for seeing just what goes on. First, just what will the "price" for the entire economy be? It will, in fact, be just what it has been all along—that which must be given up per unit of that which is gotten. Of course, now we are dealing with a combination of thousands, if not millions, of possible goods, and to obtain a price for the mixture will take both some arithmetic and some fairly strong assumptions.

We are not going deeply into the discussion of price index calculations and their conceptual as well as mechanical problems. However, it is probably a good idea to go through the construction of a simple index just so that you can see the method as well as some of the problems of interpretation when using index numbers. First, assume that you want to construct an index representing the price level for *all* goods and services in the entire economy. To keep the computations reasonable at this point, we will assume that there are only four goods and services in the economy at this time: tricycles, haircuts, black beans, and one-room apartments. For the moment, we will also assume that each of these things is completely standard within each good. Each black bean is just like every other black bean, both actually, and in the eyes of consumers. The one-room apartments are all exactly alike and have the same advantages and disadvantages of location and convenience. A haircut is a haircut. The tricycles too are all just the same—same color, speed, and quality throughout. The fact that we have made this unrealistic assumption should point out the first problem in constructing the index. Goods that have the same name are not in fact the same. They are not physically the same nor do they perform the same services for different people. What is an automobile? What is a Ford automobile? What is a Ford four-door sedan automobile?

The next problem arises because not everyone in the economy buys exactly the same items in exactly the same quantities. Each has his own set of purchases in any given time period. The "market basket" for a given year for Mr. Rockefeller is vastly different than the "market basket" for Mr. Rogers during the same time period. Who is the "average" or "typical" consumer? Is Mr. Rockefeller, Mr. Rogers, Mr. Cleaver, Mr. General Motors Corp., who? Somehow, Mr. Average must be defined and his buying habits established and measured.

Having somehow gotten over those hurdles, we now find that Mr. Average buys the following goods in the following quantities during 1971:

Item	1971 Quantity	1971 Price	1971 Total
Tricycles	3 each	$15.00	$ 45.00
Black Beans	500 lbs.	.10	50.00
Haircuts	1 each	5.00	5.00

Total 1971 Market Basket Cost $100.00

Next year, we again go back to Mr. Average, and assume that the market basket he bought last year is the same one he's buying this year. More important, we will also assume that he is getting just as much satisfaction out of this year's purchases as he got out of the same ones last year. (Both of these assumptions are fairly stout!) In any case, for better or worse, we find that our hero is now paying the following prices:

Item	1972 Quantity	1972 Price	1972 Total
Tricycles	3 each	$20.00	$ 60.00
Black Beans	500 lbs.	.15	75.00
Haircuts	1 each	4.00	4.00

Total 1972 Market Basket Cost $139.00

In spite of all of the assumptions made thus far, we still have succeeded in getting two figures representing prices in two different time periods which can now be compared. Note that for both periods, the average prices paid by Mr. Average are *weighted* by their relative importance in the total budget of the buyer. There will be more discussion on this point shortly.

We are not really all that interested in the actual price paid for the market basket. Of much more interest is how the prices have changed, specifically, how the general price level has changed. To calculate this, we divide the prices in the year of interest by the prices in the year we designate as "base," Assuming the interest is in comparing 1972 prices with 1971 prices, then the index will be:

$$\frac{1972 \text{ Market Basket Cost}}{1971 \text{ Market Basket Cost}} = \frac{\$139.00}{\$100.00} \quad 1.39$$

There are several ways that the result can be (and is) stated. First, one can say that prices increased by 39 percent. We can also say that the price index in 1972 is 139, given 1971 as base year = 100. Finally, of course, it can be said that prices are 1.39 times what they were in 1971. While this all says the same thing, it is crucially important to be consistent in the way changes are expressed.

There are some other interesting aspects of index numbers that can be seen from this simple-minded example. The average price level increased by 39 percent, true enough. But in no way does that imply that all prices went up by 39 percent. In fact, the price of tricycles went up by 33 percent, the price of black beans went up by 50 percent, and the price of haircuts went *down* by 20 percent. (Incidentally, note how well the market operated in forcing barbers to lower their ridiculous price. Unfortunately, the way our index is constructed maintaining the same market basket, any increase in quantity demanded would not show up in this time period.) This is the way a weighted average works, and while it is very useful, you must remember that many details, sometimes very important details, are hidden by the averaging process.

The same problems mentioned above plague the index makers as much in the real world as in our greatly simplified example. But once calculated, the price index can be a useful tool if its limitations are remembered.

To acquire the rest of the information we need to discuss an aggregate demand curve we need some measure of output. In this case, we will use the concept of a deflated or *real* dollar value of all goods and services in the economy. Most of you have probably forgotten, but the microeconomic demand curves were all based on quantity demanded *per unit time*. They were based on a quantity *flow*, not a stock. So it is again for the quantity demanded of total output. It is the *rate* of output we are concerned with, such as GNP or NNP in constant dollars per year. Thus, the figure we are looking for is the y we have been using to discuss the several markets.

There is one more assumption that must be made to allow a reasonably simple model. This assumption will be dropped later, but for the present assume that the economy has completely flexible prices—all prices including the wages paid to factors of production. If this is the case, then when prices go up or down because of inflationary or deflationary pressures, it really will make no difference in the buying power of the factors of production receiving wages. All prices and all wages will move together. If the price of a car doubles, the wages of people buying cars will also have doubled.

Now let's return to the *IS/LM* equilibrium illustration. In Figure 3.2, a set of curves are presented which show a given equilibrium at interest rate r_0 and output y_0. Remember that one of the several things being held constant in this analysis was the level of real balances—the real purchasing power of money. To hold this constant meant that we were holding both the stock of nominal money M, constant, and also the price level P, constant.

If the price level is varied, what happens? First, if the price level is raised, this will decrease M/P—decrease the real balances available in the economy. At any given level of real output in the economy there are now fewer balances available to perform the transactions and asset functions. There are just as many transactions, and since the average price of each transaction (the general price level) has fallen, there is no change in the purchasing power needed for this function. If the same quantity of real balances is still required for transactions purposes, and there are fewer total real balances available, clearly there will be fewer real balances for asset purposes. But people will be satisfied to hold the reduced level for asset purposes if and only if the interest rate falls—if the price of bonds increases. In other words, for any given level of real output, there will now have to be a lower rate of interest. The *LM* curve has *shifted* to the left as in LM_1 in Figure 3.2. The *higher* level of price is consistent with equilibrium in the money, bond, and goods market only with a lower level of real output (and a higher interest rate).

Figure 3.3, depicts the resulting relationship between the general level of prices and the output demanded in the economy. Starting at output level y_0 and price level P_0 (point a), we then raise the price level to P_1. *Ceteris paribus*, the output demanded in the economy will fall from y_0 to y_1 (point b). On the other hand, if the price level is lowered, real balances are left for assets purposes. These are absorbed only at lower interest rates. The *LM* curve has shifted to the right (LM_2 in Figure 3.2). The lower price

Figure 3.2
Price and Output Demanded

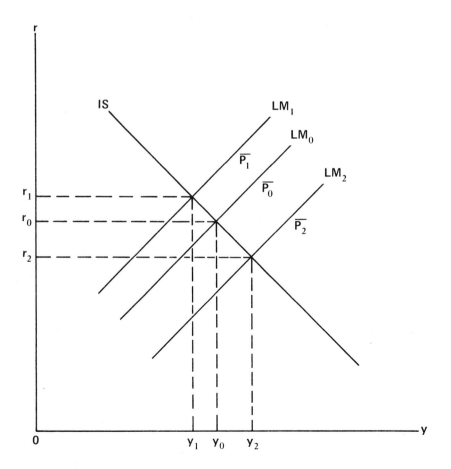

Figure 3.3
Aggregate Demand

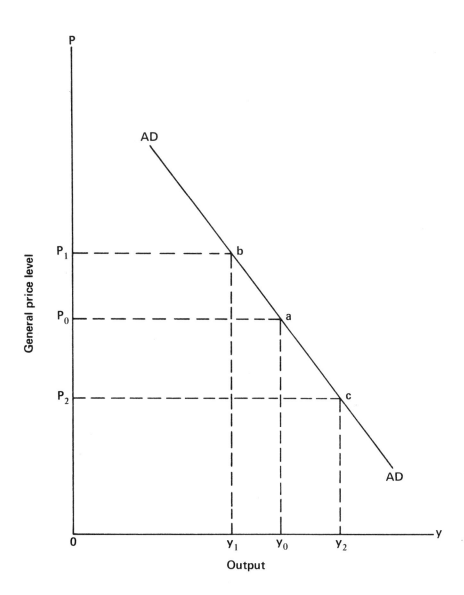

level P_2 will be consistent with a higher level of output demanded, y_2. If we vary the price level continuously, then the downward-sloping aggregate demand curve shown in Figure 3.3 is generated. Again, this reasonably complicated development makes perfectly good everyday sense. Given the stock of nominal money in the economy, and all of the variables we have discussed as being fixed, at higher prices people will be able to buy less, and at lower prices they will be able to buy more. Note, a change in the price level has not effected anything about the IS curve. It has stayed right where it was before.

In the policy book of this series, we will discuss some possible changes that might be induced in the position of the IS by a change in the general level of prices. But basically, all of the variables that are used to derive the IS function are expressed in *real* terms. Changes in price do not effect them. As stated before, if prices change, so does purchasing power. The dollar values used to quantify these variables have already been corrected for any possible price changes.

Next we develop the other side of our aggregate market—aggregate supply. In doing so, we will look at the final market in the economy, the labor market, and see what it is that will get an economic system to produce.

Chapter Four   Aggregate Supply

What will determine the level of output an economy is both capable of and willing to produce? The question itself contains the seeds of its answer. To produce anything, an economy must have productive capacity. It must have the resources, both natural and developed, capable of accomplishing such production processes as are desired by the system. Not only must the resources, or factors of production, be available, but they must also be induced to work by some means or other.

There are three conditions necessary for the production of goods. First, the factor itself must be available. Men and women must exist to perform labor. Second, raw materials of some sort must be in the picture. Third, capital goods of some sort must either be immediately available or capable of being created. In a sense, then, one could say that it is necessary for factors of production to exist in some sort of "raw" or "crude" state if there is to be any hope of production. Having the crude factors available will not assure production, however. They are a *necessary*, but not a *sufficient* condition for production. A couple of the more obvious examples of this fact can be seen in India and Brazil.

India is certainly not suffering from a lack of population, in fact, quite the contrary. But this availability of labor has not stimulated great leaps forward in material productivity. Brazil probably has more mineral wealth than any other country today, yet again, this has not (as yet) brought forth astounding increases in material production and prosperity.

These two examples point up the second necessary condition. Factors not only have to be available in a crude state, but they must also be potentially productive. The Indian slum-dweller who is incapable of reading, writing, or using the most basic arithmetic is hardly the same potential input as the graduate of even the poorest college in the U.S.A. I am *not* saying that the Indian might not be able to become productive given sufficient time and investment of educational resources. I am saying that *right now* his productive potential is vastly lower than his U.S. counterpart even though demographically, he would count as one person—one laborer. Similarly, natural resources may exist in different places and be of different qualities, or in the case of Brazil, to get at the resources is very difficult. A loom is a loom; but a loom operating in modern-day Japan is probably a very much more productive piece of capital than most looms operating today in South America. The steel factories, newly built after World War II in Germany and Japan are not the same as many of the steel factories operating today in this country. Quality, then, in the sense of potential productivity is another essential condition for output to "happen" in an economy.

Please note that to this point the necessary conditions for production have had nothing to do with the market system or any other system. What we have said applies equally to any society, even those on a subsistence level. It is in the third necessary but not sufficient condition where all the fireworks start. A country can have factors, and the factors can have good productive capacity. But unless something gives them a reason to produce—an incentive—nothing happens. When one mentions the word "incentives," backs go up in the air, and everyone starts spouting his or her favorite philosophy. This thing or idea is "right" and the other idea is "wrong." Analysis and logic take flight in absolute panic. Actually, the economist does not pretend to be an expert in *why* people do what they do. He is much more interested in the consequences of whatever actions they do, in fact, take. With that mild disclaimer, it world be useful to talk about the subject of incentives, and how economic systems differ in their view and use of incentives.

Controlled economies, that is, economies where market-type decisions are made by a controlling body or individual, still find it necessary to employ both "carrots" and "sticks" in getting factors to go to work. In this generation of new revolutionary regimes, one of the most effective carrots has been dedication to the revolutionary ideals that brought the group to power: "Do this or that because your comrades need to have you do it! Do it for the better life of your sons and daughters! You will find true freedom in working for the common good!" Do not laugh at this approach; it has and continues to work very well indeed.

The times and places this technique has been most effective should be noted, however. The first, and on occasion the second, generation of revolutionaries seems to accept this approach without too much questioning. The places it seems to work well are countries having very low initial levels of material prosperity, or at least low levels among the mass of those who carried out the revolution: "Life has been tough and poor anyway; nothing could be much worse. Therefore, let us at least suffer in the *hope* of something better in the future." Interestingly enough, revolutions have a tendency to calm down after a couple of generations, and the old fervor seems to work less well on the children and grandchildren of the revolution. If economic development has taken place as well (as has certainly been the case in Russia and some of the Eastern European countries), the old austerity does not look as good as some of the material goodies. Planners find they have more to plan, and any wrong estimates are less and less tolerated by the people. Insidiously at first, the old market begins to work itself back into the life of the economy, and later, with the blessings of those governing.

There are also many "sticks" used in controlled economies. The threat of a shot in the back of the head is an amazingly effective incentive to get people to work, and work at what "the government" wishes them to do. Concentration camps of World War II, for instance, produced many instances of gentle people doing chores that would make Nero blush in return for the privilege of staying alive. Right or wrong, this kind of stick is amazingly effective.

All kinds of other incentives can be used to stimulate production by factors. Public rewards, medals, a star on the calendar if you brush your teeth, and a public denunciation if you do not make a production quota are all inducements that can and have worked at some time and in some place. This brings us next to the incentives provided by the operation of a market system.

Whether a market system is good or bad depends a great deal on your ideas about the position of the individual viz-à-viz the world around him. If you place high value on personal freedom of action, and the right of individuals to either "make it or break it," then probably the market system has the potential to carry this out better than any other system. Note, it will not necessarily do so unless it is operating in a reasonably "perfect" manner, but it can do it.

The market rewards people by providing the vehicle for demanders of products to pay suppliers of those products. It is really no more complex than that. If people produce what other people want, everyone gets paid. The amount of the pay will depend on how scarce the item is (scarce in an economic sense), how badly people want it, how much they are willing to give up to get it. The other side of the coin is equally true; if a factor is not producing what demanders are demanding, their pay will be poor or non-existent. Thus there is both a carrot and a stick built into the system. Factors, including labor, are both led and pushed into areas of production that they are most capable of performing, as well as the activities pro-ducing the most wanted products.

Rewards paid by the market system generally take the form of money wages. To the extent that these wages are freely determined in the market-place, they will reflect all of the complex psychic factors that go into people's likes and dislikes about different occupations. It is possible, for example, that a professor might be crazy enough to accept a lower salary if the job were in southern California than he would to teach an Eskimo settlement north of the Arctic Circle. The *job* might be identical, but the conditions of the job are very different. The market would reflect these differences as well as the potential job-holders' view of the differences.

In our analysis of aggregate supply we will be looking at an aggregate labor market that, again, makes some fairly strong assumptions. We will assume that the supply of labor is an increasing function of the real wage.

Again that word *real*. The real wage is merely the buying power wage. It is calculated by deflating money wages, W, by some measure of the price level, P. In the same way that real balances consist of M/P, real wages are obtained by W/P. The way we are using *wages* refers to the *rate of pay* labor is receiving. We have not mentioned it explicitly, but you should realize that in discussing *the* wage rate, we are actually talking about some kind of average including everything from the salary of the president of General Motors to the sweeper at the corner grocery. What wage rate really represents is a *structure* of wages in individual labor markets, all of which are assumed to be in equilibrium. It does not make any difference if the rate is per hour, day, week, or year, as long as it is used consistently. Given our supply of labor, then, as the real wage rate increases, either more people will be willing to work that are not now working, and/or people that are now working will be willing to work more. In Figure 4.1, this function is shown by $N_s N_s$. Most graphs in this book start off backwards, upside down, or both, and this one is no exception. Here we show the quantity of labor, N, either supplied or demanded on a southbound axis with righthand origin o. The real wage, W/P is shown on the westbound axis starting from o. The demand curve, $N_d N_d$, is perfectly normal and shows that as the real wage rate rises (the cost of hiring rises), the quantity of labor demanded will fall. (A discussion of this demand curve, and where it comes from, is included in the next section.) Where the supply and demand curve intersect, we have equilibrium in the labor market with quantity ob both demanded and supplied at an average (aggregate) wage of oa. Everyone wanting to work at this wage can find a job, and everyone wanting to hire at this wage can find employees.

Since we are basically discussing a production economy, the labor must be combined with some kind of capital if it is to be productive. Again, conceptually we lump all the capital resources of the economy together into one grand and glorious overall productive plant.

A plant without labor has zero productivity; man is still an essential part of the productive process. As labor is added to the existing capital stocks, the product in the economy starts to climb. Assuming the capital stocks to be fixed at any moment in time, then the more labor we add, the more product we will get, *but at a decreasing rate*. The *Law of Diminishing Returns* comes into play. Marginal additions of labor contribute to an increase in total product, but these increases get smaller and smaller as the capital stocks become more fully utilized. In Figure 4.2, this production

Figure 4.1
The Labor Market

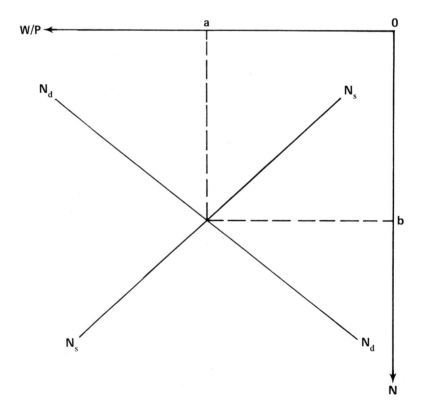

Figure 4.2
The Aggregate Production Function

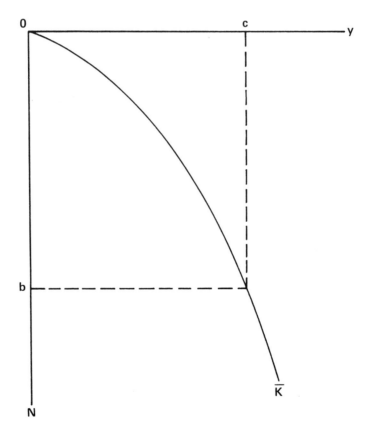

function is illustrated. Note that the production curve bellies toward the output, *y* axis indicating the decreasing marginal product gain from positive increments of labor. In this graph, we have taken the equilibrium quantity of labor, *ob*, added it to the existing capital stocks in the economy via the production function, and have derived a level of output *oc*. Thus we have *one* level of output supplied—one point on our aggregate supply curve.

But where does price come into the picture? At what price level will this level of output be produced? To answer these questions see Figure 4.3. Figures 4.1 and 4.2 have been combined in Figure 4.3 along their common southbound axis representing employment of labor. In addition, a general price level axis has been erected northbound from origin *o*. This gives us a northeast quadrant with price level and output on the respective axes, and a northwest quadrant with price level and real wages on the two axes. In this quadrant, there are several rectangular hyperbolas constructed, each of which represents a constant money wage, given changing levels of prices and real wages.

In the previous discussion of the demand for money, when we multiplied *graphically* the value of one axis times the value of the other, the product equals the area of the rectangle made up by the two axes and perpendiculars erected from the axes to the point in question. See Figure 4.3. On the vertical axis, we have the value of *P*, the price level. On the horizontal axis we have the value of *W/P*, the real wage. If the value of the *P* - axis is multiplied by the value on the *W/P* - axis, the result is,

$$P \times W / P = W$$

In other words, the values of areas in the northwest quadrant are equal to nominal money values. When the value of real wages is equal to *oa* and the price level is equal to oP_0, the value of rectangle oP_0fa is equal to the value of *money wages*. Later in this discussion, we are going to be interested in what happens when prices and/or real wages change and money wages remain constant. Therefore, we will need curves in the northwest quadrant which will represent constant money wages.

From the study of money or from basic geometry, a rectangular hyperbola has the following characteristics; any point on a rectangular hyperbola will generate a "box" underneath it of equal area to any other box constructed from any other point. Thus, in Figure 4.3, the area, and hence the money value, of rectangle oP_0fa is equal to rectangle oP_1ed. The

Figure 4.3
Aggregate Supply

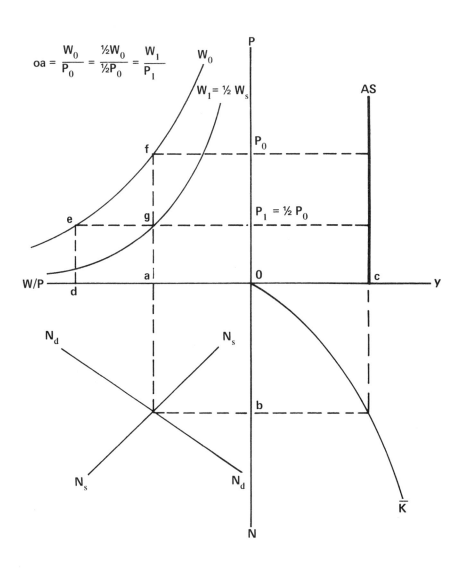

$$oa = \frac{W_0}{P_0} = \frac{\tfrac{1}{2}W_0}{\tfrac{1}{2}P_0} = \frac{W_1}{P_1}$$

money values of wages represented by points along this curve are all equal to each other. A change in the money wage means that there is a shift from a point on one curve to a point on another.

Assume that in Figure 4.3 real wage *oa* is composed of money wage W_0 and price level P_0 or in symbols, $oa = W_0/P_0$. Given the production function in the southeast quadrant, this real wage will provide an equilibrium level equal to *ob* and an equilibrium level of output of *oc*. Therefore, output supplied at price level P_0 will equal *oc*. Next assume that the level of prices falls to one half its P_0 level. Remember the assumption that wages and prices were completely flexible and would therefore move together in an inflationary or deflationary situation. Therefore, if P_0 decreases to one half its initial level, W_0 will also fall to one half its initial level. What does this do to the level of real wages? The answer, as is obvious, is *absolutely nothing*! Real wages will stay the same.

$$oa = W_0 / P_0 = \tfrac{1}{2}W_0 / \tfrac{1}{2}P_0 = W_1 = P_1$$

This means there is nothing to disturb the initial equilibrium in the labor market. The quantity of labor demanded and supplied will stay the same at level *ob*, and output will stay the same at level *oc*. Therefore, output *oc* will also be consistent with price level P_1 as well as price level P_0. The same situation will occur if the prices increase. A doubling of the price level will double the money wage level as well, and real wages will again stay the same.

This produces an aggregate supply curve completely independent of the price level. No matter what the price level does, output will remain the same. Output depends on the level of capital stocks and their quality, as shown by the production function, and by the quantity of labor that is willing and able to work. This, in turn, depends on the level of real wage which is independent of the price level, given completely flexible price movements in the economy. As we all know, in our economy at least, this is a far cry from the truth insofar as the short run is concerned. Given enough time prices will adjust, but the time periods can be long and tough on unemployed factors of production. This whole issue will be taken up in the next chapter.

One final note of caution should be added before closing this section of the discussion. If you have been following closely, you have probably determined that there is a relationship between the slope of the production function and the value of the demand for labor real wage. The slope of the production function represents the *rate* at which production increases when additional labor is added to the process. From micro theory, you already know, that given our assumptions about perfect markets, factors will receive wages (real wages) equal to the value of their marginal products. However, the slope of the production function will not represent the real wages earned by labor at different quantities of labor. The slope of the production function will give you the value of product added to output by the marginal addition of labor input. But there is no way of saying that this marginal increment is produced by just the labor. On the contrary, the marginal increment is from better utilization of existing capital stocks, as well as the efforts of labor. Capital must also receive its return if capital stocks are to be renewed, maintained, or increased. The real wage rate of labor must be something less than the value of incremental output created by adding labor to a given capital stock.

In Chapter 5 we combine the aggregate demand and aggregate supply and see how the whole thing works together.

Chapter Five

The System

Initially we will put aggregate supply and aggregate demand together to see how the economy would work if all of our assumptions about perfect markets were correct. No, this isn't a waste of time because by doing it this way, it will give us a series of benchmarks on which to build more realistic conditions. Without this "ideal," it would not be possible to evaluate just what the problems of imperfect markets actually are. You're almost through the hyper-dry stuff so bear with it just a bit longer.

In Figures 5.1a and 5.1b, we have merely combined the aggregate supply diagrams of the last chapter with our previously developed aggregate demand. Assume the government fouls up the comfortable equilib-

Figure 5:1a
The Aggregate Economy

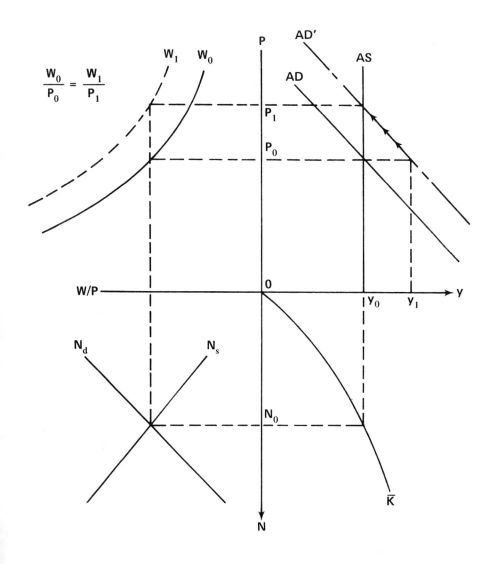

Figure 5.1b
Aggregate Demand

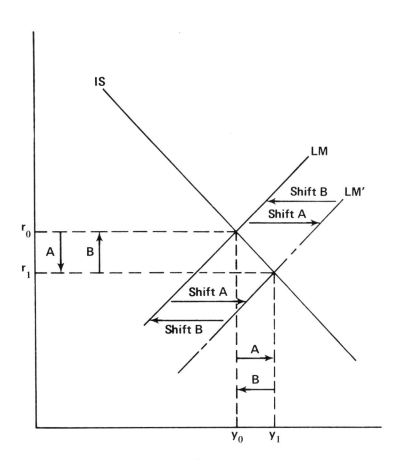

rium by printing up a big batch of new money and throwing it out of airplanes to the general public. Initially, real balances will have increased because the M of our M/P has increased. More real balances in the economy means that *ceteris paribus*, people will try to spend more on both goods and bonds. The increased demand for bonds will tend to raise the price of bonds, or lower the interest rate. Thus, any given level of interest will be consistent with higher levels of output, or any given level of output will be consistent with lower rates of interest. Either way it is viewed, the *LM* curve will have shifted to the right. The last time we shifted *LM* to the right, we did so by conceptually allowing price levels to change—the P in our M/P. In so doing, we developed the aggregate demand curve, i.e., the relationship between output demanded and the price level. Nominal money stocks were one of the things held constant in generating the demand curve. Now we have shifted *LM* due to a change in the money stocks, holding prices constant for the moment. This shift in *LM* shifts the demand curve. It produces an increase in the whole demand schedule rather than merely a movement along the demand schedule. In Figure 5.1a this shift is shown as *AD'*. Note that it merely reflects what happened in the aggregate demand (*IS–LM*) sector. At the price level P_0, the output demanded will now be equal to y_1 rather than y_0. Without a change in the price level, this would mean that the new quantity demanded, y_1, would be greater than the quantity supplied, still y_0, and there would be shortages in the economy. This is basically the same kind of analysis that you studied in microeconomics. This shortage generates upward pressures on the price level; people have more buying power than there are goods *at the existing structure of prices*. The attempt to use this additional buying power results in prices being bid up, and the prices of goods and services go up.

As prices start to climb, the value of M/P starts back down. In this case, it is the increase in the price level that is reducing the level of real balances. P is going up while M is staying constant. The *LM* curve moves back to its original position at *LM*. Because this shift is the result of a price level change, we are now talking about a movement along the demand curve as illustrated by the arrows moving northwest along *AD'* in Figure 5.1a. At price level P_1, prices will have increased in an exact proportion to the increase in the money supply. Wages, too, will have gone up in proportion to the increase in prices. Real wages have remained constant as per the previous discussion, and therefore, aggregate supply has not changed. It is precisely because of this completely inelastic supply that price, and price alone, has made all of the adjustment to the initial impact of an increased nominal money supply.

This is the classical case described by eighteenth century economists as being the workings of a market system. If prices are left alone to find their levels, output will not be affected. Unemployment (involuntary unemployment) of any factor is impossible under this system. At any moment in time, given any particular level of capital stock in the economy, the level of output will be determined by the real wage of labor which is independent of the general price level. All aggregate demand can do is change the general price level, not the level of output.

It is worthwhile to investigate a few other examples of this model in operation with perfectly operating markets. Many times it is stated that economic growth takes place when the stocks of productive capital increase in an economy. Without worrying about *how* this takes place for the moment, assume that such an increase in productive capital did, in fact, take place. See Figure 5.2 to determine how this model illustrates the result. Once an increase in capital stocks has taken place, there is no necessary reason why aggregate demand need be affected. It may or may not be. But an increase in the productive capacity of the economy has definitely happened. Given the same input of labor, the total product will increase. Given the situation as illustrated, the gains in the economy from this capital stock increase would accrue to the holders of capital. (Of course, these holders of capital may be laborers as well.) The real wages in the economy have not changed and, therefore, the buying power of labor has not changed. A more typical and probable case is illustrated in Figure 5.3.

In this case, the increase in capital stocks is accompanied by an increase in the productivity of labor itself. This means that any given quantity of labor will gain a higher real wage than previously. In other words, the demand for labor has increased. In Figure 5.3, this is shown by a movement of N_d to N'_d. In this particular example, the money wage of labor falls from W_0 to W_1. It just as easily could have actually risen. The important point is that real wages definitely increased. W_1/P_1 is definitely larger than W_0/P_0. Total production goes up from y_0 to y_1 and employment actually increases in this instance from N_0 to N_1. This case would be particularly appropriate if the increase in capital were in the form of human capital. By definition, this kind of investment improves the productivity of the labor force.

Figure 5.2
Increase in Capital Stocks

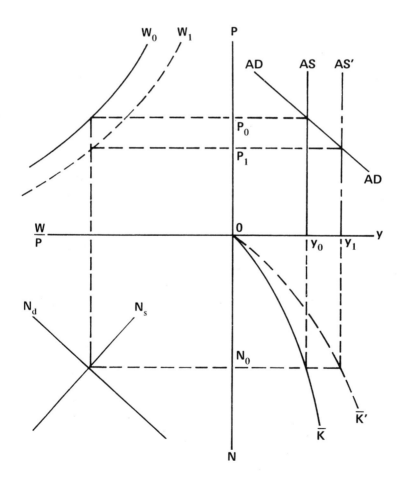

Figure 5.3
Increased Capital Stocks With Increased Labor Productivity

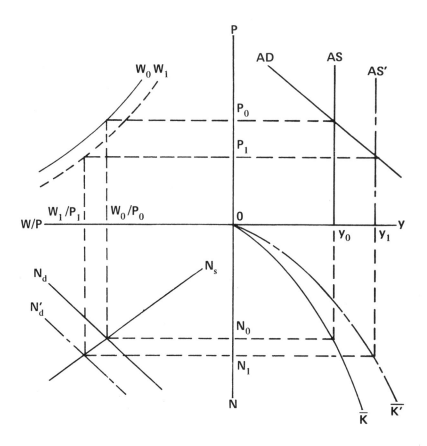

Next we more closely approach that strange situation known as the "real world." In most market economies, the ideal of free flexible prices and markets operating in a purely competitive fashion is quite a distance from reality. To see the nature of the problem, let us assume that in the short run no wages are flexible in a downward direction. Prices and money wages can go up with no problem, given stimulus; but when deflationary pressures are exerted, nothing happens, that is, nothing happens in the form of lower prices.

The first thing that changes is the shape of the aggregate supply curve. In Figure 5.4, this problem is illustrated. As usual, start with the full employment equilibrium at price level P_0, money wage W_0, real wage W_0/P_0, labor employment of N_0, and output of y_0. Assume that something happens to cut back on aggregate demand, such as the money supply being reduced. AD shifts back to AD'. If all wages and prices were flexible, the price level would drop to P_2 money wages would adjust, and the level of real output would remain the same. There would be no unemployment, merely lower prices and money wages. Buying power wages would remain the same.

Next assume that money wages are fixed. Workers refuse to take a cut in their money income even though the price level has fallen. As the price level falls, we move along the constant money wage curve W_0. Price level is falling and money wages are constant, therefore real wages are increasing. But as the real wage rate increases, the quantity of labor demanded decreases and the quantity supplied increases. If the quantity demanded is less than the quantity supplied, and if the real wage is held above equilibrium, then the quantity demanded will be the one that counts. Employers will be willing and able to hire only the smaller quantity regardless of what quantity of labor people are willing to supply. As a result, there will be unemployment of labor by the amount that N_{d1} exceeds N_{s1}. The employed working force will drop from N_0 to N_1. Output will drop from y_0 to y_1. Note that while we are talking about unemployed labor, there will be unused plant capacity—unused capital stocks—as well. In our example, y_1 is now the result of price level P_1, and y_1 is less than the full employment output level y_0. In effect, what happens is the development of an elastic "tail" on the downward portion of the aggregate supply curve.

If wages were also rigid in an upward direction, there would again be a problem. Graph this situation for yourself, and what you will find is a

Figure 5.4
Rigid Downward Wages

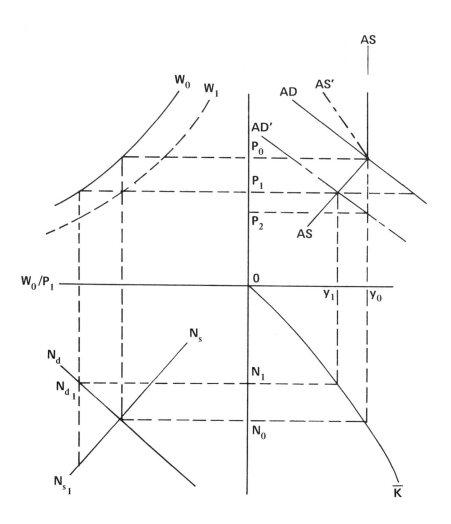

backward bending upper portion such as *AS'* in Figure 5.4. In this case, were the price level to stray at all from P_0, there would automatically be unemployment until wages could adjust. Actually, from a practical stand-point, neither wages nor prices remain fixed over a long term if pressures are there to change them. Both are "sticky," but sooner or later, if the pressures persist, the wages and prices will begin to move. The problem, however, is precisely this "stickiness."

Without complete flexibility, unemployment will take place during the adjustment process. This can and does create substantial hardship for those that are unable to find work. It is primarily this problem of unemploy-ment, along with the problem of stable prices that has caused government to take an active role in the economy. It is that role which forms the basis for the discussions of the next chapter. The mechanics of government and foreign trade operations will be covered as a transition to the next book in the series on macroeconomic policy issues. Thus, Chapter 6 will give you the tools to understand quite a bit about the nature and potential solu-tions to many of our economic ills.

Chapter Six

Govern- ments and Foreigners

One of the primary reasons for studying macroeconomics is to try and develop models which simulate, but at the same time simplify, the real world. These models can then be used to assist in the prediction of future events. Note, I said *assist*. There is no model which can be used with complete assurance of accuracy. The use of models is still a combination of science and art, and art plays a very heavy role. It has been previously mentioned that the pure perfect market world, which has been the primary thrust of this study thus far, does not really exist. Because of imperfections in both markets and man's understanding of them, the government, particularly the federal government, has come to play a role of increasing importance in manipulating the system. The specific policy issues of government intervention will be covered in the macro-issue books of this series, but now it is important to discuss where the government fits into the scheme of the model thus far developed.

Government economic policy is loosely divided into monetary policy and fiscal policy. The distinction between the two is not clear-cut because what starts out to be fiscal policy, in some instances, may well end up by affecting the money supply. But basically, fiscal policy involves the government's use of taxation and government expenditures while monetary policy involves changes in the money supply.

As far as monetary policy, and its effects on the model are concerned, we have previously given examples. An increase in the nominal stock of money means that purchasing power in the economy *apparently* increases. The *LM* curve shifts outward to the right which shifts the aggregate demand curve outward to the right. If the economy is operating at full capacity, the price level will go up in proportion to the increase in the money stock, thus offsetting the initial apparent purchasing power increase. If the economy is operating in any elastic portion of the supply curve, the economy can be stimulated to increase aggregate output. Again, these movements and their significance will be dealt with in much more detail in the next book.

To see what happens when government either changes the rate at which it taxes, or changes the rate at which it spends resources, we go back to the demand for goods. In Figure 6.1, we have redrawn the goods market, but this time something has been added. Remember that when we discussed saving, we noted that saving amounted to a "leakage" of spending in the economy. Resources spend on consumption become income for someone else. Resources spend on investment also become income for someone else. But saving *without* investing amounts to a leakage in this spending flow. If saving increases, that is, if the proportion of income not spent increases, then aggregate demand for goods and services decreases as well. In our diagram, the *IS* curve shifts back to the left so that given the conditions in the money market, output demanded will fall. The aggregate demand curve will also shift back to the left.

An increase in *taxes* is analytically similar to an increase in saving. Taxes, too, represent a leakage from spending in the economy. Taxes are not the same thing as government spending. Taxes are the collections of governments. Granted, governments have a fairly strong tendency to spend

Figure 6.1
The Effect of Taxes

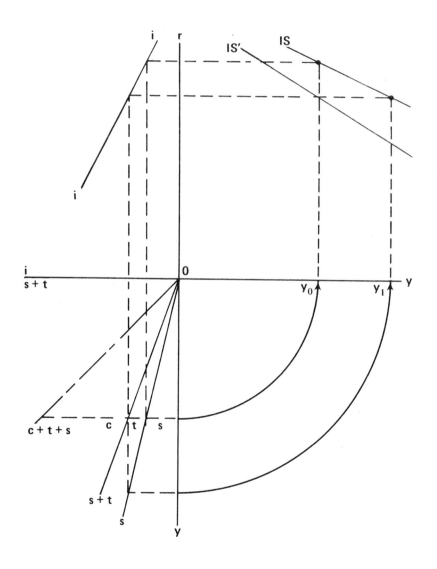

at least what they take in, and often more. But the "taking in" is a leakage. Until these tax resources are spent, they represent a reduction in the purchasing power of the civilian sector. The results of an increase in (or the establishment of) taxes is shown in Figure 6.1. The s line rotates clockwise and becomes the $s + t$ line. The same results would have occurred if the saving function itself was increased. The IS function shifts back to the left which, in turn, reduces the total aggregate demand for all goods and services. Obviously, then, the government has a powerful tool to influence the level of economic activity and the general level of prices. Again, this tool of policy will be examined in detail in the upcoming book on policy.

As indicated, governments do tend to spend the resources they acquire, and this shows up in our goods market. Government expenditures represent another use of goods. Whereas taxes were a leakage, expenditures are an injection of resources—a spending back into the economy. In this way, they are analytically similar to investments except there is no reason to believe that government expenditures will have any necessary relationship to the interest rate. To show the effect of government expenditures, refer to Figure 6.2. We have included the resources spent by government in the northwest quadrant along with investment expenditures. Note that there is nothing to indicate that the amount the government spends has anything to do with the interest rate. All that has been done is to tack on a level of g for each possible interest rate. This method is sufficient for analysis, but there is one big danger that should be pointed out; just because government expenditures are shown in the investment quadrant, do not make the mistake of thinking that all government expenditures are investments. They most assuredly are *not*. True, the government does make investments—resources put into projects which will yield increased future productivity—but government also spends money on consumption items which are lost and gone forever once spent, and which have no possible positive impact on future productivity.

One other economic concept, that of the government spending multiplier, is illustrated by Figure 6.2. The concept is that if government spends a dollar, the dollar again becomes income for others. If no one saves anything, that one buck could create a bunch of income for others as it made the rounds. The lower the marginal propensity to save (the higher the marginal propensity to consume), the higher will be the multiplier. In this case, expenditures of g result in an increase in the output demanded of

Figure 6.2
Government Expenditures

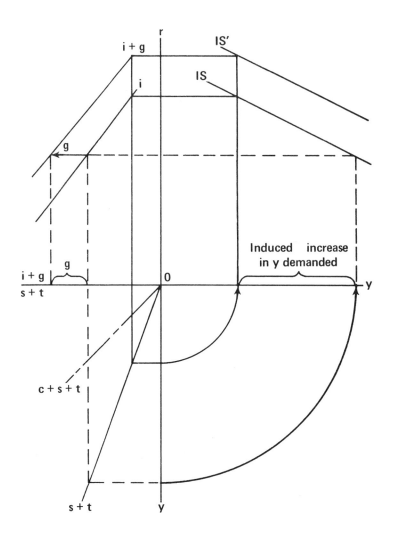

several times this amount as illustrated in the diagram. The effectiveness of the multiplier effect cannot be denied, but it is often vastly overstated for reasons that, again, are made clear in the next book. Finally, note that an increase in private investment of the same magnitude as g would have the same multiplied effect on output demanded. An increase in the marginal propensity to consume would also do the same thing.

The final item that will be discussed in this volume is the effect of foreign trade on our economy. Up to this point, we have been discussing a circular flow economy in which nothing could come in from the outside, and nothing could leave. Given this situation, our "no free lunch" axiom mentioned in Chapter 1 held perfectly true. What was consumed domestically had to be produced domestically. What was produced domestically had to be consumed domestically. Trade between countries expands the possibilities for both production and consumption. In the same way that comparative advantage works between individuals and between regions of a country, so it also works between nations. There is no reason why any country has to be absolutely the best at producing different goods and services. As long as the relative cost of production of different goods varies between countries, all potential trading partners can gain from trade.

How are imports and exports shown in our model? Imports are analytically similar to another leakage of domestic spending power. Resources paid out of the economy do not become purchasing power for others in the economy. Of course, this assumes that the import in question actually replaces some item of domestic manufacture. In Figure 6.3, we have added imports to our $s + t$ line, and as before, the result is to shift back the IS function and, therefore, decrease aggregate demand.

A couple of points should be made before going further. The way this model has been developed, it has been implied, although not stated, that each new leakage discussed necessarily added to the leakages already existing. This is, of course, untrue. There is no reason to believe that increased taxes, for example, will come only out of consumption expenditures. In fact, it is more likely that both consumption and saving will be reduced if taxes are increased. Increased taxes will, therefore, not have all of the impact that they would have had were consumption the only item that decreased. Similarly, there is no reason to believe that increased imports would necessarily displace dollar for dollar domestic production. The complete ramifications of this point will be covered in the issues book.

Figure 6.3
Imports

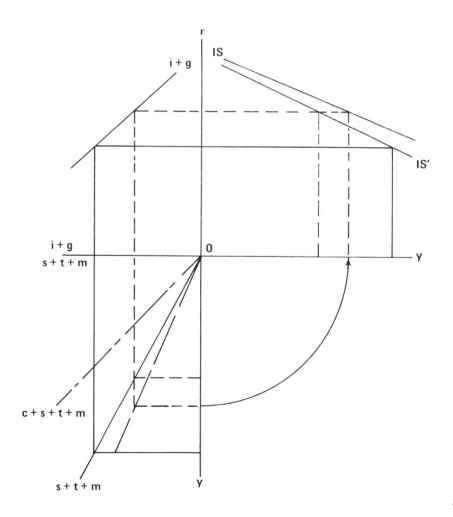

Figure 6.4
Exports

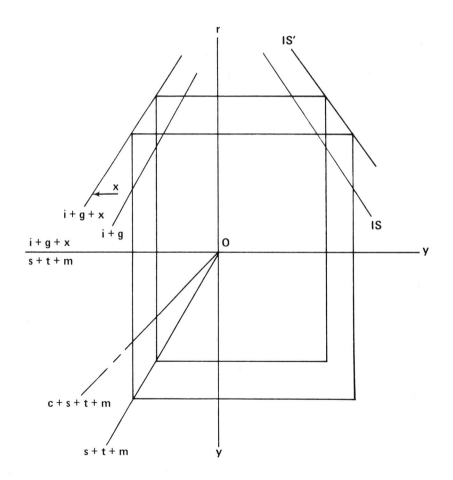

Since imports have been shown in the saving sector, it is obvious that exports will be shown in the investment sector. Exports, like investment, represent another potential use of the economy's production. Now we can consume our goods, invest them, or sell them to someone outside the domestic marketplace. We can also export them. In Figure 6.4, the $i + g$ line has been increased by the amount of our hypothetical export increase. The $i + g$ now becomes $i + g + x$. There is no reason why, in this model, the level of exports would necessarily depend on the rate of interest. Therefore, we assume independence between the two. Like government expenditures, the x quantity is merely added to each possible combination of investment and interest rate. The new function is parallel to the old. This tends to shift the *IS* function to the right, thus increasing the aggregate demand in the economy. Figure 6.4 traces through the geometry of this action.

This simple model gives you most of the tools needed to gain a basic understanding of the policy issues facing our government and citizenry today. The mechanics are tedious but necessary, and if you will just force yourself to really understand the material that has been covered in this brief text, then understanding the policy problems of the next book will be a piece of cake. I know it boggles the imagination to consider it, but you might even *enjoy* the upcoming section of the course!